TREASURES

IN THE KREMLIN

TREASURES IN THE KREMLIN

PAUL HAMLYN · LONDON

ARTIA · PRAGUE

PROGRESS · MOSCOW

TREASURES IN THE KREMLIN

INTRODUCED AND EDITED BY ACADEMICIAN B. A. RYBAKOV
PHOTOGRAPHS BY KAREL NEUBERT
INTRODUCTIONS TO SECTIONS AND CAPTIONS TO PHOTOGRAPHS ARE BY MEMBERS OF THE STAFF OF THE ARMOURY N. V. GORDEEV, A. A. GONCHAROVA, L. V. PISARSKAYA, L. P. KIRILLOVA, K. V. DONOVA, AND E. I. SMIRNOVA

PUBLISHED JOINTLY BY PAUL HAMLYN LIMITED, LONDON,
ARTIA PUBLISHERS, PRAGUE,
PROGRESS PUBLISHERS, MOSCOW
DESIGNED BY JAROSLAV ŠVÁB

PRINTED IN CZECHOSLOVAKIA
S 1654
FIRST PUBLISHED 1962
SECOND IMPRESSION, REVISED, 1964

THE ARMOURY — *ORUZHEINAYA PALATA* — OF THE MOSCOW KREMLIN originated in the 15th century from the treasures of the grand princes. It is one of the oldest museums in Europe.

The present Armoury building (1851) stands on the hill where Moscow had its beginnings 800 years ago. In 1147, Prince Yuri Dolgoruky, son of Vladimir Monomakh, feasted his allies there, and the local inhabitants must have eyed with curiosity the wonderful gifts of the Chernigov princes, which included such a rarity as the fleet-footed cheetah. Three hundred years later, the Moscow princes built the 'Treasury', a repository for their valuables—ancient heirlooms and the presents of Oriental and Byzantine potentates. The Treasury was housed in a new building in 1485, almost simultaneously with the erection of the Kremlin walls.

The name *Oruzheinaya Palata* first occurs in a description of a fire in 1547; it may have originated in 1511 with the institution of the office of 'Armourer'; this was filled by a grandee who supervised the making and keeping of royal arms and accoutrements.

For the last two centuries the Armoury has been an amalgamation of court workshops and repositories dating to the 16th and 17th centuries. It is now a showroom of the work of famous Russian artists, goldsmiths, silversmiths and armourers who knew the secret of damascening steel; collections of regalia, resplendet thrones, rare saddles, harnesses and coaches, royal dress, and a magnificent collection of English and German silverwork, possibly the only one in Europe, consisting of the presents of European monarchs.

The royal treasury suffered greatly from fires and the 'time of troubles' (1606—11), when artistic plate was minted into coin for Polish and Swedish troops and mercenaries, and when a succession of upstart rulers plundered and sold the valuables accumulated by generations of princes. Later, the tsars themselves gave freely from these collections. What has come down to us is only a small part of the riches once kept in the treasuries and workshops of the Kremlin.

Peter the Great brought the various repositories together and deposited in the Armoury many of the objects captured in the fighting against the Swedes.

A plan to turn the Armoury into a public museum was timed for the inauguration of Moscow University in 1755, but the idea was rejected by court circles and was realised only in 1806. During the Patriotic War of 1812 its collections were removed, and returned to the present building in 1851. It was erected in the pseudo-Russian style by K. A. Ton, the architect of Nicholas I.

The Armoury became a truly popular museum only after the October Revolution in 1917:

church treasures, small collections, and recent finds were added to it, and it was opened to the public. The new exhibition shown here in Karel Neubert's superb photographs reflects contemporary scientific understanding of the history of civilisation.

In its five centuries the Armoury has seen many talented and learned men, among them the armourers Nikita Davydov, Grigory Vyatkin and Afanasy Vyatkin; the icon painter Simon Ushakov and the engravers A. Zubov and I. Zubov; from 1655 to 1680, Bogdan Khitrovo, a sensible boyar, was in charge of the Armoury. The prominent Russian historian S. M. Solovyov was one of its directors in the second half of the 19th century.

A visitors' book dating from the 15th century would contain the names of foreign diplomats, travellers, statesmen and military commanders, such as the Venetian Ambrogio Contarini; the imperial ambassadors, Siegmund Freiherr zu Herberstein (1518 and 1526) and Hans Kobenzl (1576), the English navigator Richard Chancellor seeking the North-east Passage (1553), the papal legate, the Jesuit Antonio Possevino, the Englishmen Jerome Horsey and Giles Fletcher, the Patriarch Jeremias of Constantinople (1589), Duke John of Holstein (1602), the Dutch cartographer Isaac Massa, the Frenchman Jacques Margeret (1606) and many others who have left vivid accounts of this ancient treasure-house, and of the *Granovitaya Palata* (the 'Faceted Hall'), where valuables were displayed when the court was held.

'In the course of eight days we were shown the sights of the city, in particular the treasure-house at whose gate stood two lions in effigy: one apparently of silver and the other of gold. It is just as difficult to imagine as to describe the riches contained in the treasure-house . . .'

'The repository of royal robes was likewise of incredible value.'

'The arsenal is so big and so richly supplied as to allow the arming of 20,000 horsemen.' (Don Juan the Persian, 1599.)

The exhibits of the State Armoury illustrate a thousand years of Russian history and art. The earliest objects are from a Byzantine treasure-trove discovered in the village of Bolshoi Kamenets, Kursk Region, in 1927. It includes a tall silver jug wrought in Constantinople in the 5th century A.D., with a likeness of the nine Muses in relief. How did it find its way to the heart of the forest-steppe? The answer is evidently in the campaigns of the ancient Sclavinae and Antes against Byzantium, which were especially frequent in 530, during the reign of the Emperor Justinian. The spoils of the successful campaign were found buried in the territory of the Severyane tribe, near the present-day town of Sudzha.

Many of the exhibits are connected with the feudal Rus of the 12th century. A silver chalice from Pereyaslavl-Zalessky, apparently dating back to 1152, the year of the founding of a white stone cathedral in the town, is linked with Yuri Dolgoruky, the founder of Moscow. A big silver loving cup which was once taken by the Tatars to Sarai Berke, their capital on the Lower Volga, dates from the same period. On it is a circular inscription providing valuable information about its original owner. It says: 'This cup belongs to the Prince Vladimir Davydovich, and whosoever drinks from it, to him the best of health, and all praise to God and to our Lord the Grand Prince.'

Vladimir Davydovich was the Prince of Chernigov, an ally of Yuri Dolgoruky (ruled from 1139); in 1151 he was killed in a battle in Yuri's defence. This inscription corrects a persistent historical fallacy: it proves that the rulers of the separate lands were titled 'Grand Prince' as far back as the first half of the 12th century.

Two famous helmets are of great historical value. It has long since been established that one of them, found on the scene of the battle of Lipitsa (1216), belonged to the Prince Yaroslav Vsevolodovich, who fled, leaving his accoutrements behind. Recent attempts to date the helmet to another period are groundless: it was made by Russian craftsmen in the early 13th century.

The other helmet, made in Constantinople in the 12th century, may also have belonged to a Russian prince; a special type of helmet, similar to the wide-brimmed pyramidal Byzantine helmet of the Armoury, occurs several times in the ancient illustrated *Radzivil Chronicle*, a copy of earlier 12th and 13th century manuscripts. In the drawings, the wide-brimmed plumed helmet stands out among the thousands of other conventional Russian helmets of that time. The first such helmet is worn in 1149 by Prince Andrei Bogolyubsky at the battle of Lutsk; a few pages later his brother, Mikhail Yuryevich, is pictured in 1169 wearing a similar broad-brimmed helmet topped with a faceted spike. We know that Yuri Dolgoruky's sons were connected with Byzantium; in mid-12th-century Rus such a costly helmet, 'a hat of the Greekish land', as the *byliny* put it, could have been in the possession of Andrei and Mikhail and its curious shape may have attracted the attention of court artists. It has long been a relic: 17th-century descriptions said it was 'unarmed', i.e. not adapted for wearing in battle.

The painter Victor Vasnetsov used exhibits in the Armoury, the helmet in particular, for his well-known canvas *The Three Bogatyrs:* it is worn by the bogatyr Dobrynya Nikitich.

Among the splendid objects made by Russian craftsmen of the 12th and 13th centuries is a costly piece of golden finery which belonged to a Ryazan princess; it is ornamented with gems of many colours, filigree and unfading multicoloured enamel. It is part of a treasure-trove discovered in the former capital of Ryazan principality in 1822, which included head-dress pendants and necklace medallions with images of Christian saints, possibly the patron saints of the members of the princely family: Boris and Gleb, Maria, Varvara and Irina. In the 12th and 13th centuries, several Ryazan princes bore the name of Gleb. These valuables were apparently hidden in the ground from the Tatars, who destroyed the town in 1237. Fine enamelled wares were no longer made after the Tatar invasion: the art of cloisonné had been lost.

Such objects carry us back to the early principalities of the North-east, to the flourishing Rus before the Mongolian invasion, a period the Russians recalled with pride under the Tatar yoke: 'O, brightly radiant Russian land! Thou art full of everything and art endowed with many marvellous beauties!'

The next group of relics takes us to another period, when the small Moscow principality made a courageous effort to muster the forces of the Russian lands for the life-and-death battle against the Tatars in Kulikovo Polye in 1380.

Some of the objects are connected with the men who in the 14th and 15th centuries conducted Moscow's policy of integration (the Metropolitans Pyotr and Aleksei, the Grand Prince Ivan III); others illustrate the results of this policy, when towns in every part of the young state sent to the new capital their sacred relics and the personal belongings of celebrated rulers whose lands were integrated in the Grand Principality of Moscow.

Ancient inventories indicate that a *kalita*, a morocco leather pouch embroidered in silver, was once kept at the Armoury. It had belonged to Grand Prince Daniil, a son of Alexander Nevsky. Could that reputed miser, Daniil's son Ivan Kalita ('money-bags'), have been nicknamed after this pouch? Unfortunately, it disappeared from the Armoury several centuries ago.

It is possible that the golden hat of fine Central Asian design belonged to Ivan Kalita (1327—41) himself. There are indications that it was a gift from Khan Uzbek to his vassal. In the late 15th century it was remodelled into the so-called 'Cap of Monomakh'.

A vestment adorned with pearls and embossed plaques belonged to the Metropolitan Pyotr, Ivan's associate, who had cast in the lot of the Orthodox Church with Moscow (1322). A gorgeous vestment studded with pearls, gilt plates and enamelled plaques dating to the pre-Mongolian era had belonged to another prominent 14th-century churchman and political leader, the Metropolitan Aleksei of Moscow, who was also Dmitry Donskoi's tutor. He came from a rich Chernigov family and apparently used ancient boyar costumes in the making of his vestments.

The well-known reliquary of Dionisy, Bishop of Suzdal, (1383) is an interesting historical reminder of the turbulent period of struggle for the office of Moscow Metropolitan which followed upon Aleksei's death. Dionisy had opposed Moscow's policy of unification, and obtained the canonisation of the Suzdal princes. He was then involved in various schemes to secure the office; the candidates travelled to Constantinople by different routes, poisoned their rivals, and offered bribes to the Patriarch. From Constantinople Dionisy brought home a variety of 'relics' in a silver casket. The bishop flattered the men among the Patriarch's retinue who provided the 'sacred relics', and called them 'God-fearing fathers who live like angels'. He did not forget to praise his Prince, Dmitry Konstantinovich of Suzdal (Dmitry Donskoi's father-in-law), who had ordered the precious casket.

When the Suzdal-Nizhny Novgorod principality was integrated with Moscow, the churchmen immured the Constantinople relic in the cathedral wall, and it was only in 1401 that the casket was found and sent in solemn procession to Moscow, which Dionisy had vainly fought all his life.

The embossed setting of the Russian-made icon 'Our Lady of Vladimir' is connected with Metropolitan Foty (1408—31), a learned Greek. He also brought from Constantinople a vestment with embroidered portraits of the Byzantine Emperor and the Moscow Prince Vasily I, Dmitry Donskoi's son (1389—1425).

Moscow's war trophies of the 15th century are represented by an excellent hunting spear which belonged to the Tver Prince Boris Aleksandrovich (1425—61). The splendour of his court rivalled that of the major courts of Eastern Europe; his court chronicler, the monk Foma, anticipated the 'Third Rome' theory, comparing Tver with Rome and Constantinople. The socket of the hunting spear is covered with silver leaf on which are engraved eight compositions: a young man conversing with a princess; hunters killing a wolf and a bear; a man holding out a goblet to another; scenes of a struggle, whipping, and offerings of some sort of fluid in a pail . . . These scenes are echoed in some parts of *The Story of Pyotr and Fevronia*, a 15th-century Russian tale, and in the legend of the founding of a Tver monastery, but they are not identical with any extant writings.

In 1430, Boris was invited, among other kings and princes, to the coronation of Witold, Grand Duke of Lithuania. This excellent hunting-pole may have been ordered for the occasion, for paleographic data place it in the second quarter of the 15th century.

Many objects are connected with the court and church activities of the Grand Prince Ivan III, sovereign of the vast territory between the Baltic and the Urals, the White Sea and the 'Wild Steppe' in the south. The Kremlin halls were gutted by many fires and repeatedly plundered, yet we have splendid things of Russian and West European make from that interesting period. They include a curious German 'kur', a vessel in the shape of a cock; Italian carvings in ivory; and monumental 'sions', sacred utensils for high mass reproducing the well-proportioned forms of 15th-century Russian architecture; and the bindings of bulky volumes with exquisite filigree patterns.
We can readily understand why the Crimean khans wrote florid letters to Ivan III asking for accoutrements and utensils 'of Moscow make'.

Exhibits from the 16th century not only show the skill of the craftsmen who worked in the various court 'halls' but also recreate a picture of Moscow's extensive commercial and diplomatic ties with remote countries of West and East.
Exquisite fabrics from Iran, skilfully fashioned weapons from Turkey, rare porcelain from distant China and objects from Renaissance Europe adorned with drawings from ancient mythology, all flowed copiously into the Armoury to lie side by side with the richly ornamented handiwork of craftsmen from Moscow, Tver, Novgorod, Pskov and Smolensk.
Exhibits of the 17th and 18th centuries make the Armoury a kind of memorial museum.
On the one hand, there are the things produced in the Kremlin at the Armoury, the Gold and Silver Halls, and the Stables, by famous Moscow craftsmen who proudly marked their names on the exquisite handiwork rivalling Turkish, English, Iranian and German wares.
Situated between Europe and Asia, Russia was developing a style of her own. Articles of Moscow make were appreciated abroad. The Armoury is a memorial to several generations of celebrated Russian craftsmen who made arms, costly utensils and harness.
On the other hand, the Armoury is a museum of Russia's tsars and nobility. It would be a prodigious task indeed to list and describe the men and women whose personal things are now part of this unusual museum. Mention has already been made of what was ordered by Ivan III, or Ivan the Great, as he was known to his descendants. He was a sedate, intelligent ruler of integrated Rus; East and West were amazed not only at the expanse of his subject lands and boundless despotic power, but also at the brilliance of his court.
Rather strangely, almost nothing in the way of personal belongings has come down to us from his son, Vasily III, the last Grand Prince of Moscow (1505—33), who was as great a lover

1

2

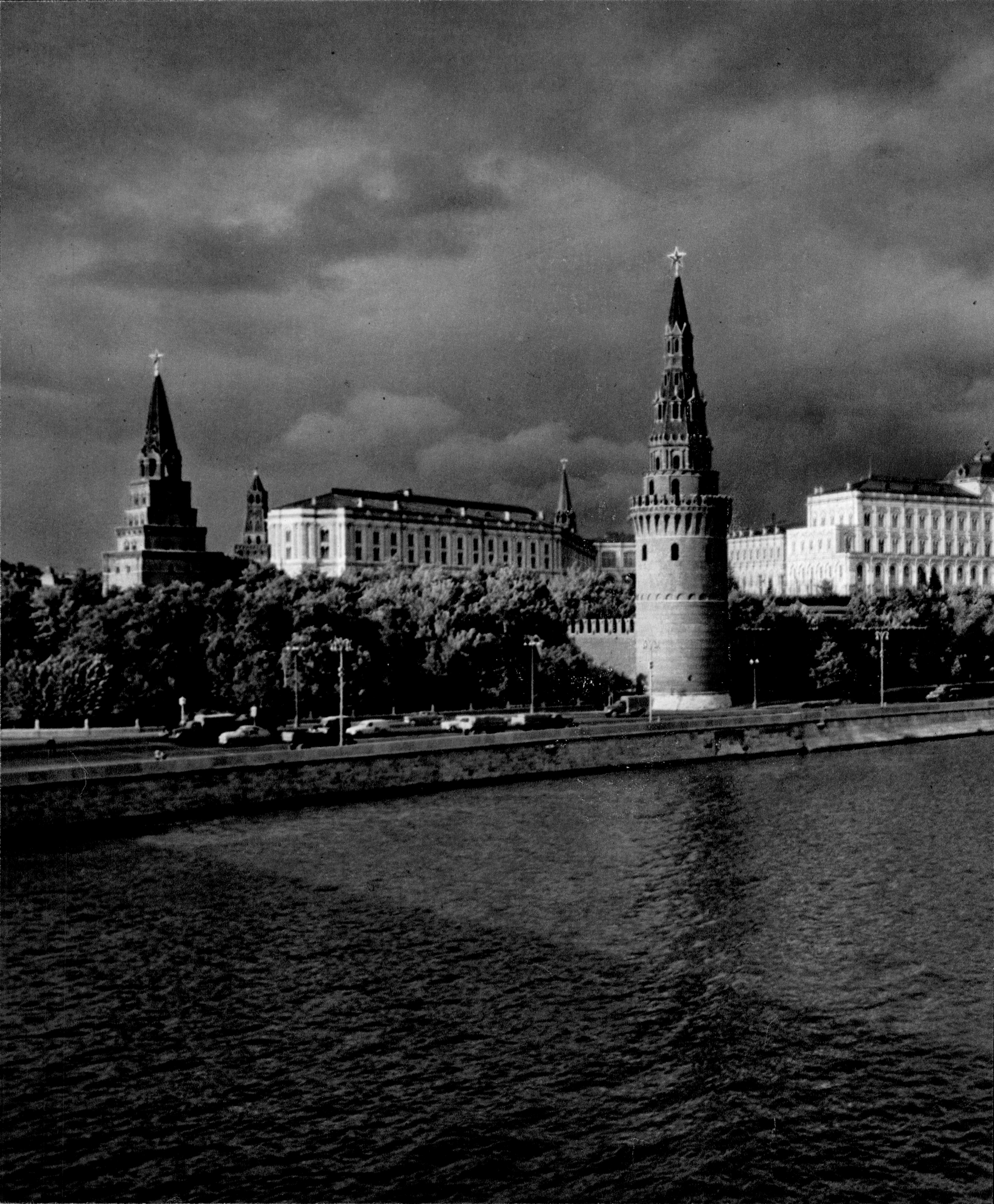

3

of court splendour as his father. But many exhibits bring to mind the latter's terrible son, Ivan IV (1547—84); they amplify our picture of his troubled but picturesque period.

Several things take us back to the time of Tsar Boris Godunov (1598—1604), whose palace stood very near the present site of the Armoury, by the Kremlin's Borovitskiye Gate. This colourful and vigorous ruler was somewhat overshadowed by foreign intervention and the large-scale peasant war, as well as by the villainies attributed to him.

The genius of Pushkin restored the memory of Boris Godunov. He is a source of historical interest because almost a century before Peter the Great he was 'opening a window into Europe'; he sent young men to study in England, attacked the troublesome nomads of the steppe, promoted Russian education and did his utmost to heal the wounds inflicted by the unbridled despotism of Ivan the Terrible.

The objects belonging to the first Patriarch of Rus, Iov, date from this period.

Among the most precious relics are the weapons of two men who in the 'time of troubles' organised and led the people in the fight to expel the invader from Moscow and the rest of Russia. They are Kuzma Minin of Nizhny Novgorod, and Prince Dmitry Pozharsky. A monument to Minin and Pozharsky (1818, by Martos) stands by the Kremlin; they are dressed in the classical robes of antiquity, following the prevailing style. Their swords are on display at the Armoury; Pozharsky's once belonged to Sultan Ali, and Minin's was made in Egypt, by 'Master Ahmed of Cairo'.

Several objects are linked with the early members of the Romanov dynasty: the weak-willed and passive Mikhail (1613—45), and Tsar Aleksei (1648—76), who was nicknamed the 'most peaceable', but who actually spent his life fighting wars, suppressing popular uprisings and struggling against the despotic Patriarch Nikon. The latter had proclaimed the doctrine of 'two luminaries': like the two celestial luminaries, the Sun and the Moon, he said, there were two terrestrial powers — the spiritual power of the Patriarch, radiant as the Sun, and the temporal power of the Tsar, glittering with reflected light. The 'most peaceable' dealt severely with Nikon (1658), revealing the full force of Russian absolutism of the 17th century.

Exhibits of the 17th century introduce a wide circle of persons, among them the chief of the Armoury, the nobleman Khitrovo.

The period of Peter the Great, who built a special museum for Russian war trophies, is reflected not only in the objects connected with his victories in the field, but also in his belongings, such as his childhood sleigh. There are also toys and children's clothes dating from earlier periods.

The 18th century is the last one amply represented in the Armoury. Of special interest are the personal things of the 'merry queen' Yelizaveta (the Empress Elizabeth), who preferred Russian-style Moscow to pretentious Petersburg.

The last of the Romanovs added little to their family treasure-house, and their additions made no difference to its basic character.

From the days of Ivan Kalita to 1917 the treasury of the grand princes and later monarchs was a court museum reflecting the history of Russian craftsmanship through the prism of royal activities. The Armoury was a sort of supplement to coronations, jubilees and court days and was designed to be a constant reminder of the greatness and antiquity of Russia's royal house.

The Great October Revolution preserved all the collections of the Armoury intact, and turned it into a truly popular museum. All the treasures of the ancient Kremlin (mainly in the sacristies of its cathedrals) were transferred to the Armoury, enriching its collections with fine pieces dating back to between the 12th and 18th centuries which had scarcely ever been on show before.

The Armoury is now an important scientific institution, a centre of comprehensive research into Russian antiquities, yielding information about historical persons, Russian and foreign craftsmen, and important events of the past.

The great crowds—Muscovites, visitors from other parts of the Soviet Union, and foreign tourists from every continent—testify to an undying interest in these art treasures.

B. A. Rybakov,

Member of the Academy of Science of the U.S.S.R.,

Member of the Academy of Science of Czechoslovakia

4

5

The collections of this section comprise over 4,000 objects, a part of the rich possessions of Muscovite princes and tsars. The earliest date back to the 13th century.

Side-arms include almost every type used in the old days—battle-axes, maces, clubs and spears. A unique collection of guns and pistols dating from between the 16th and the 18th centuries illustrates the evolution of firearms over 300 years. There is also a variety of defensive garments ranging from the quilted cloth helmet, the 'kuyak', to coats of plate and ring mail.

The greater part are decorative arms made by Russian and foreign craftsmen. Among the former are celebrated Russian craftsmen who worked at the Armoury in the 17th century: Nikita Davydov, who made arms for more than 50 years; the Vyatkin brothers, Grigory and Afanasy; Konovalov; and Konon Mikhailov; and the 18th-century gunsmiths Pyotr Lebedev, Grigory Permyakov, Ivan Lyalin, Ivan Pushkin and many others. Some of the exhibits are presents brought by the ambassadors of Western emperors and kings, and potentates of the Moslem East. Almost every object is ornamented with gold and precious stones—diamonds, rubies and emeralds.

There is a big collection of Russian standards from the time of Ivan the Terrible, some of which were carried in his campaigns against Kazan and Astrakhan; the banners of Yermak, reminders of his victorious campaigns; and the banner of Kuzma Minin and Dmitry Pozharsky. There is another big collection of banners from the time of Peter the Great—relics of the Northern War and the decisive victory at Poltava.

I. ARMS AND ARMOUR

6

7

8

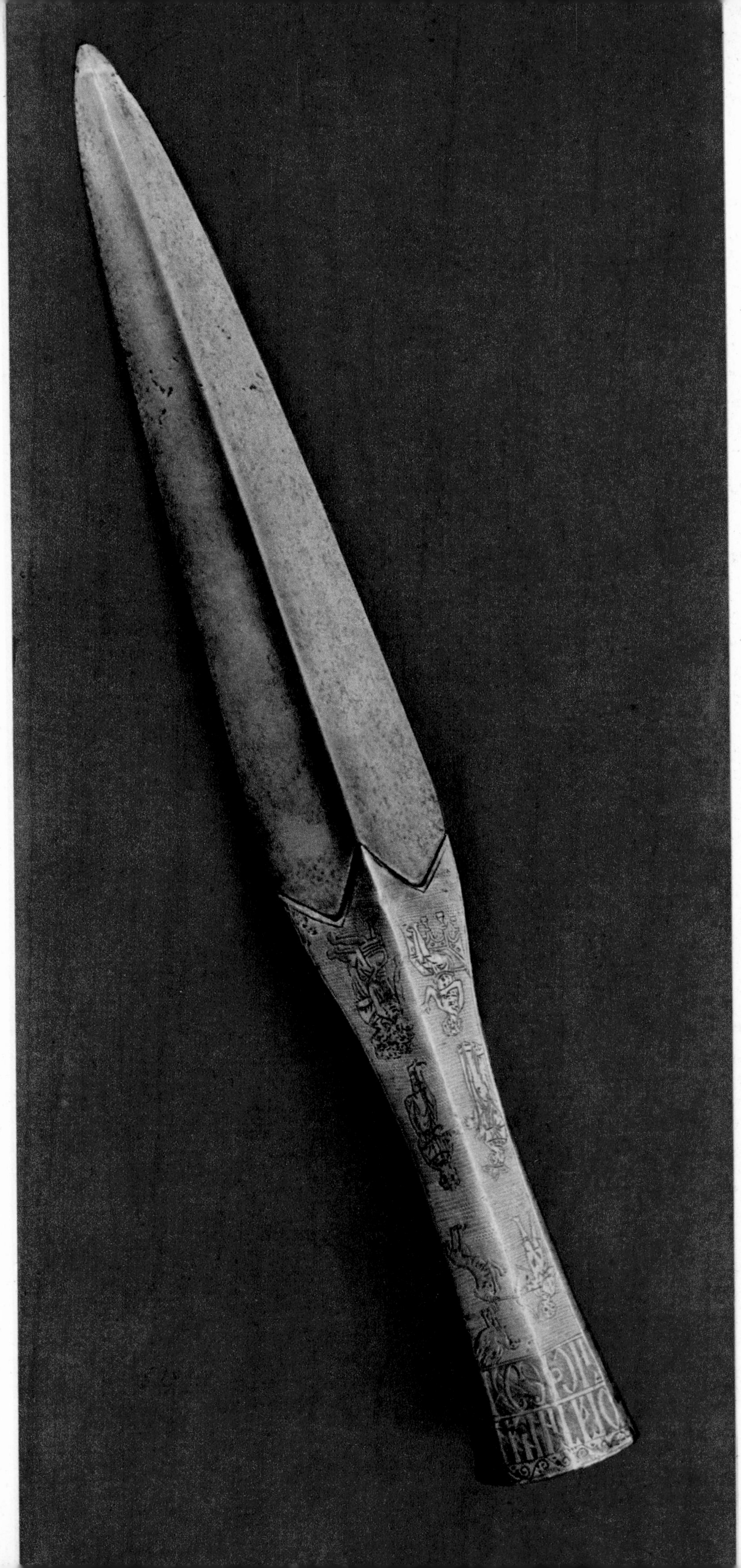

9

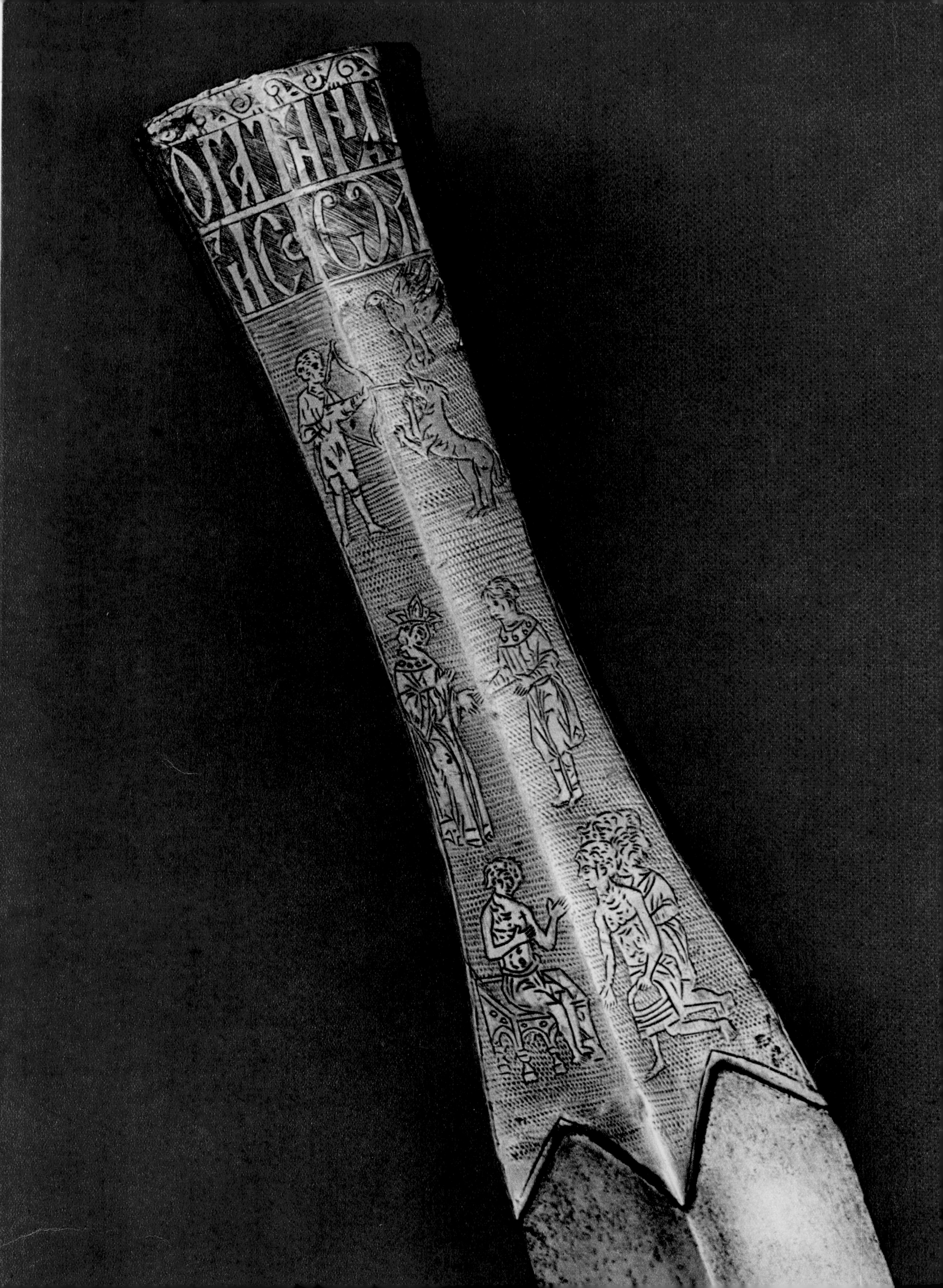

13

15

16

17

18

19

20

22

23

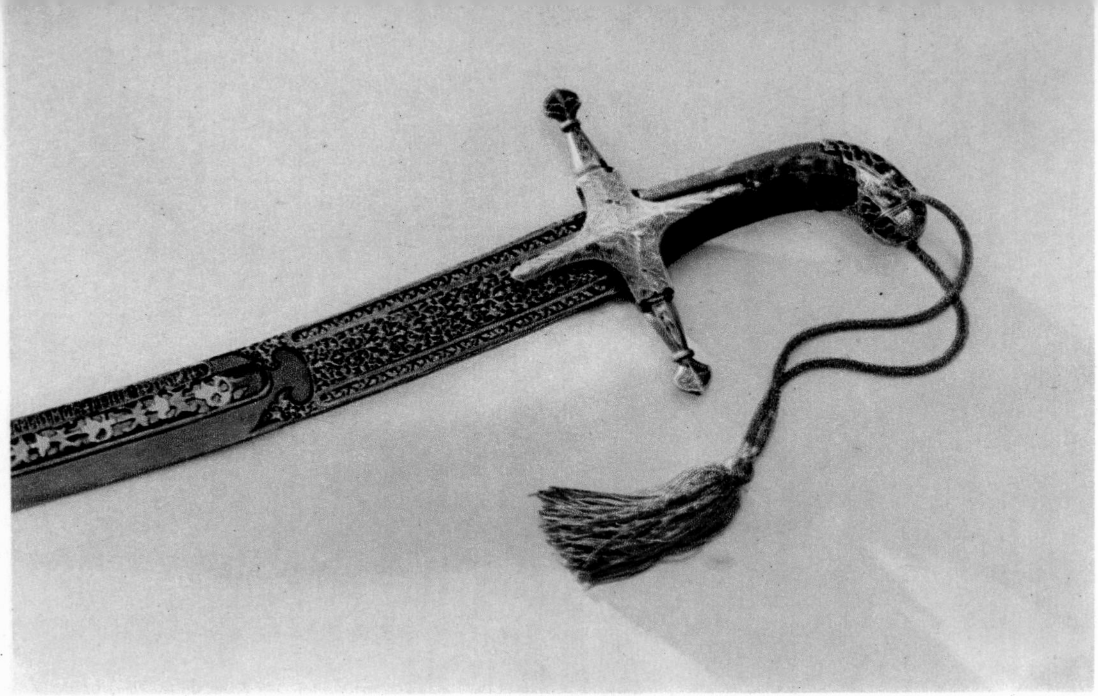

24

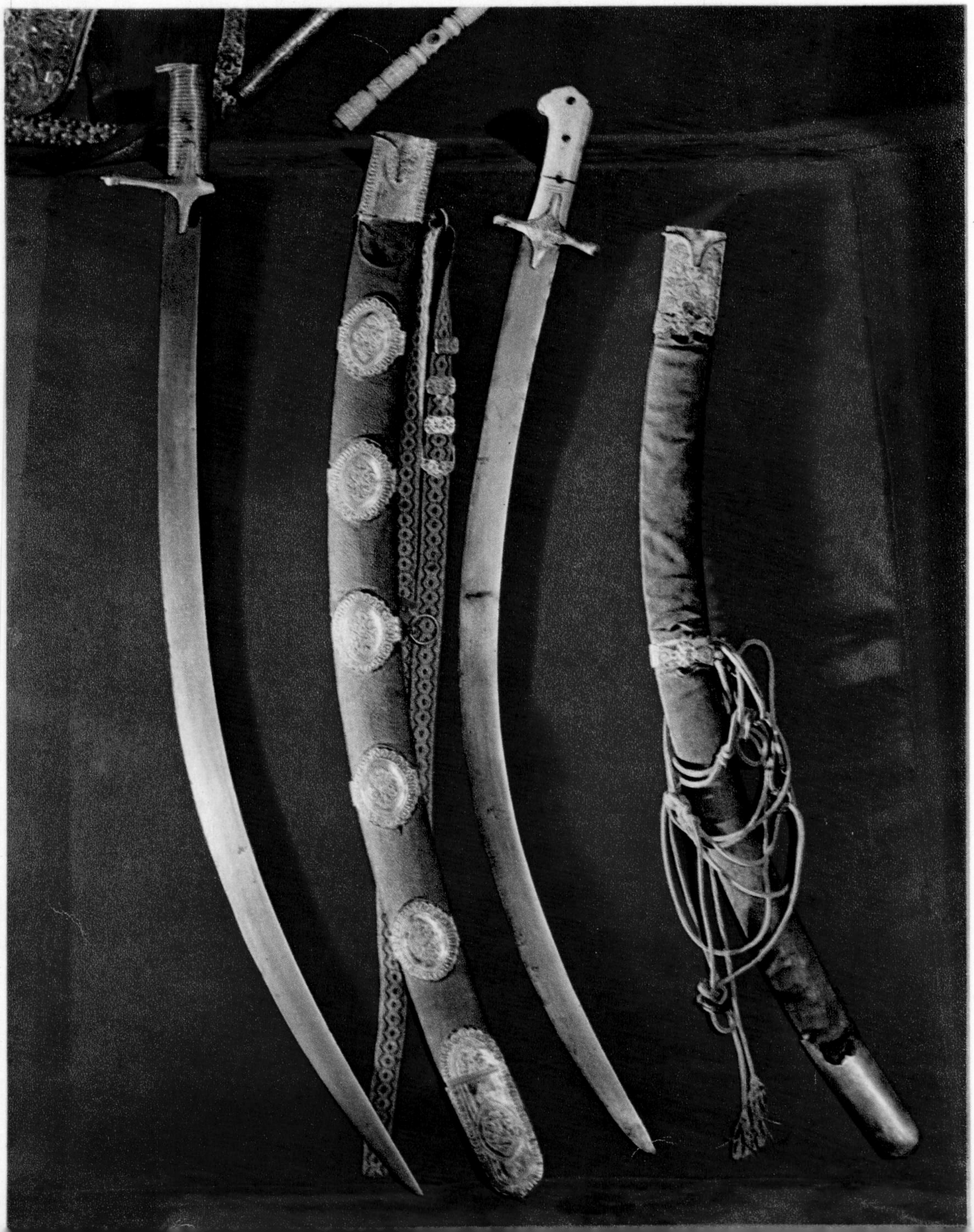

25

26

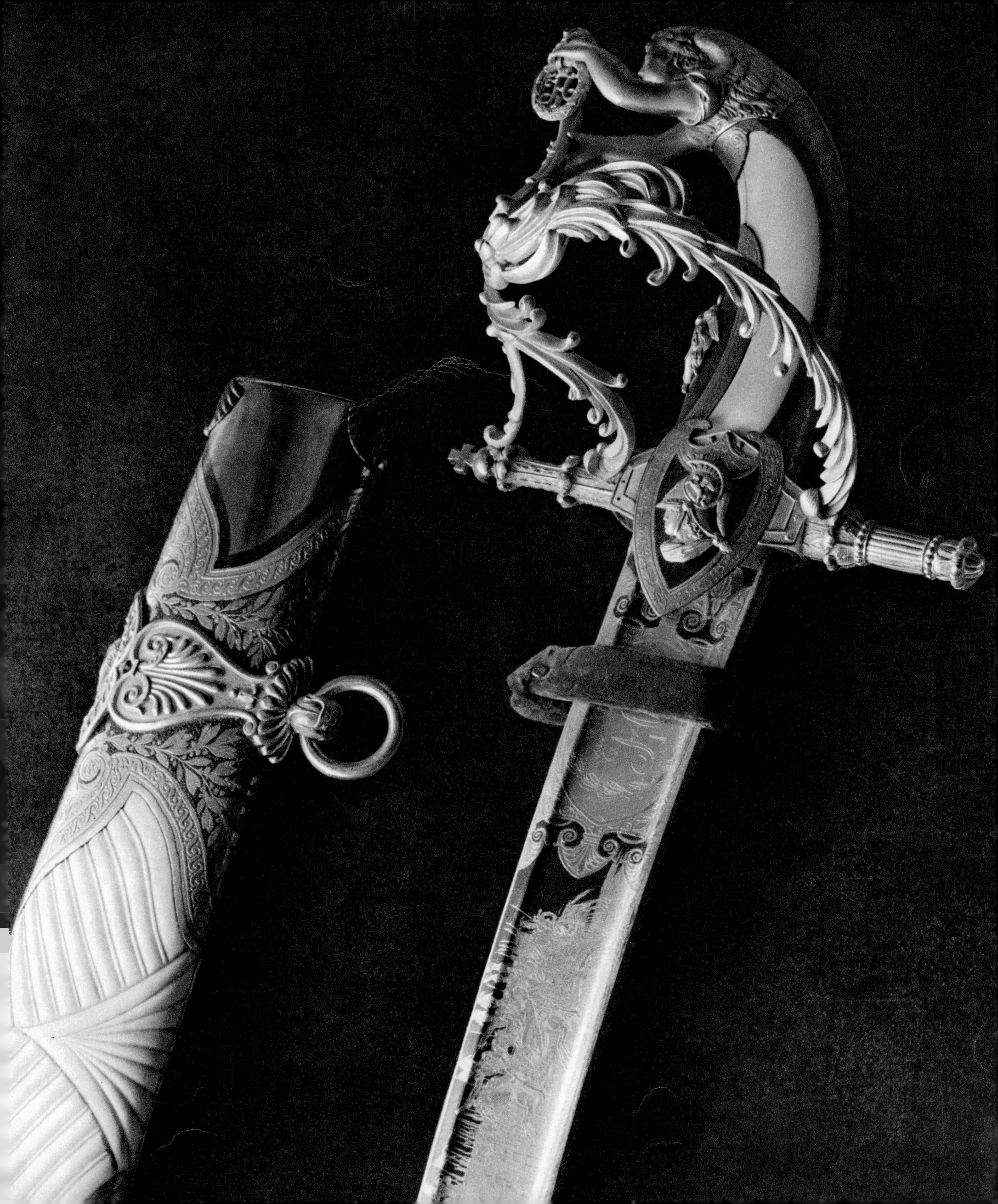

28

29

30

31

32

Pride of place among the countless unique treasures of the Armoury goes to ancient regalia (crowns, mounds, sceptres, thrones and staffs), all invaluable monuments of the history, culture and skill of Russian, Oriental, and Western craftsmen from the 13th to the 17th centuries.

These gorgeous costly things were used on state occasions, coronations, and receptions of ambassadors, and were an important part of the pomp and ceremony of the court to which Rus attached great political significance.

Many of them, like the 'Cap of Monomakh', Tsar Mikhail's 'great regalia', and the 'diamond throne', represent the best examples of work in filigree, niello, enamel, brocade, and embossing; they are done in the style of the period, and are world-famed.

The enduring artistic value of these objects, some of which are shown in this book, indicate that they were created by talented folk craftsmen. They were, as Maxim Gorky put it: '. . . the potters, blacksmiths, goldsmiths, men and women weavers, stonemasons, carpenters, carvers in wood and ivory, gunsmiths, painters, seamstresses and tailors, and in general all the handicraftsmen, the people who made the beautiful things that fill the museums and gladden the eye.'

The treasures of the Armoury, created by the people, but inaccessible to them in the past, have now become national property.

II. REGALIA

33

34
35

36

37

38

39

40

41

43

Russian gold and silverware made in the period from the 12th century to the early 20th century and the various things used by court and church are invaluable monuments of original Russian art. The objects dating from the 12th to the 15th centuries are exquisite, simple in design, modest in ornament and perfect in execution; they give an idea of the artistic culture of Kiev and Vladimir-Suzdal Rus, which subsequently became the foundation of early Muscovite art.

Most of the objects on display were made in the workshops of the Kremlin in the 16th and 17th centuries, when Russian decorative and applied arts flourished. At that time, the best craftsmen were employed at the Kremlin. They possessed a wide range of techniques, and introduced elements of folk art into court styles to produce their fabulous masterpieces. Objects from the 16th century ornamented with fine niello tracery, pastel enamels and excellent repoussé work are outstanding. Those of the 17th century generously adorned with gems, pearls and bright enamels of many colours are a striking study in luxuriant and varying ornamentation. In the 17th century, Yaroslavl, Nizhny Novgorod and Kostroma were also famous for their silverware. Solvychegodsk was famed for its enamels. In the 18th century Petersburg became the jewellery centre. In the 19th and early 20th centuries, the wares produced by the Russian firm of Fabergé were valued all over the world for their fabulous intricacy and richness.

III. RUSSIAN GOLD AND SILVERWARE

44

ΜΡ
ΘΥ

45

46

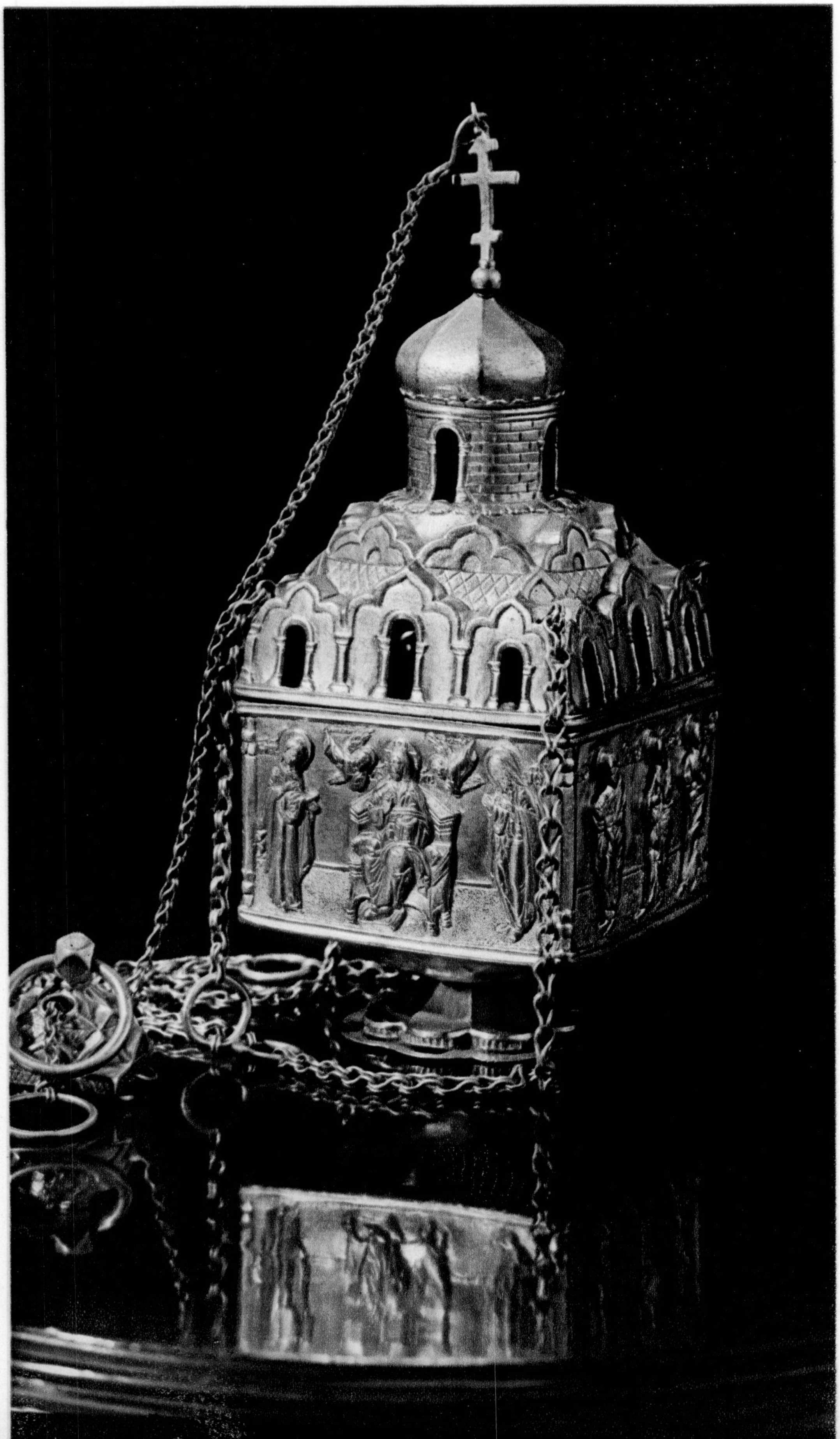

51

52

53

54

55

57

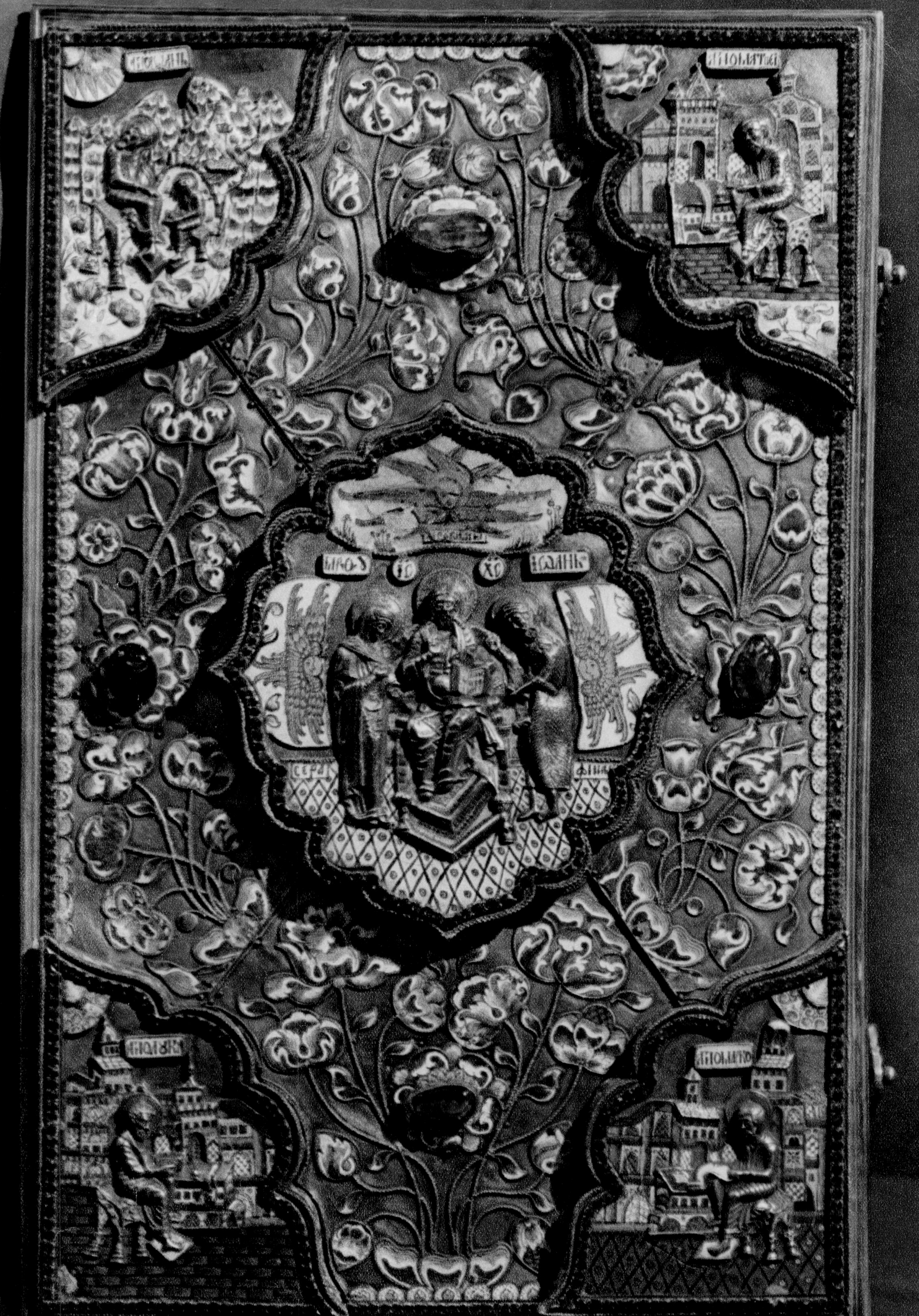

58

59

60

ПРОХОРЪ

62

64

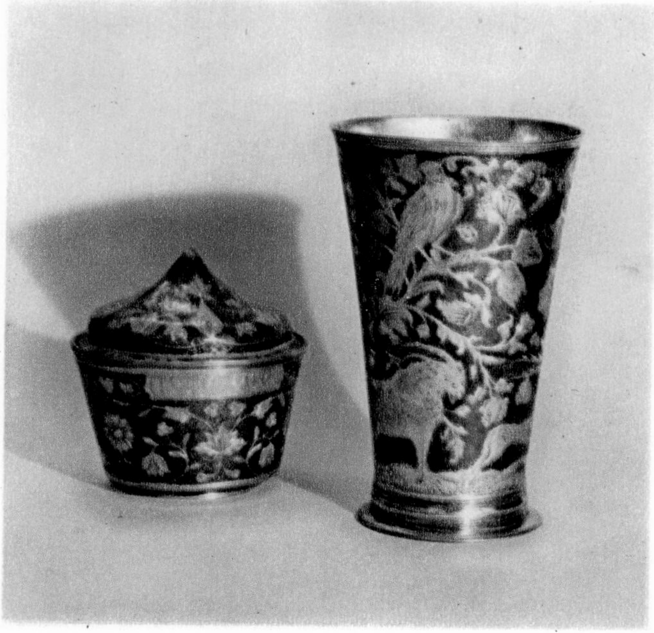

63

65

66

67

68

69

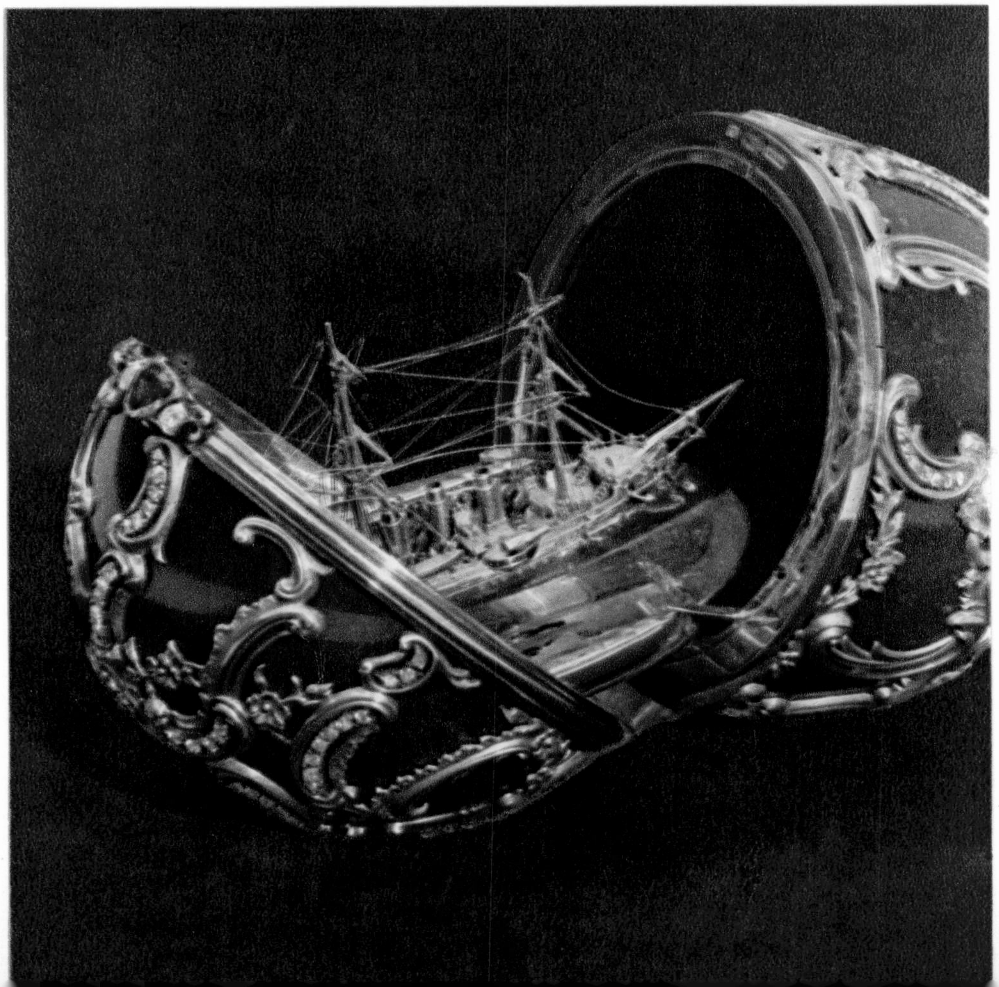

The coaches and decorative harness, like other collections of historical objects at the Armoury, are of enormous artistic value. They illustrate the pomp of the Russian court from the 16th to the 18th centuries. These objects were important as decorations at royal processions and receptions of ambassadors, to which Rus attached great importance.

Most of the harnesses were made by Russian craftsmen in the 16th and 17th centuries, and present a great variety of original patterns and figures. Prominent among them are those made by I. Popov, L. Mymrin, S. Fedotov, and L. Afanasyev, who were employed at the workshops of the Moscow Kremlin.

Exhibits of Iranian and Turkish make dating back to the 16th and 17th centuries are costly and highly picturesque, revealing exquisite artistic judgment. 17th-century Chinese objects reflect the style of the period in the applied arts. The saddles produced by Andreas Mackensen, who lived in Danzig in the second half of the 17th century, are of excellent quality. They were all gifts brought to Russia by ambassadors and trade representatives. The Armoury's collection of coaches is the world's biggest and oldest. It traces the evolution of the equipage from the primitive cumbersome carriage of the 16th century to the refined vehicles of the 18th. In the collection are the best type of coaches from Russia, Poland, England, France, Germany and Austria.

IV. DECORATIVE HARNESS AND COACHES

70

71

72

73

76

77

78

79

80

81

82

83

The collections of fabrics and costumes of the Armoury have world-wide importance: they are rare evidence of artistic weaving from many countries of the East and the West between the 14th and the 18th centuries. There is an especially full collection of Turkish, Italian, French and Russian fabrics, and a unique collection of gorgeous Italian velvets.

The collections are not made up of fragments of lost or unknown objects, but of complete sets used by clergy and laity: the dazzling vestments of tsars and patriarchs; caparisons and fur sleigh-rugs, beautiful table-cloths and bench covers. Secular costumes show the change in cut and style from the 16th to the 18th centuries. Most of the things are precisely dated, and linked with the name of their owner or particular event, all of which enhances their historical and artistic value.

Many of the exhibits are interesting examples of fancy Russian embroidery: they are skilfully embellished with intricate patterns in multicoloured silks, gold and silver thread, precious stones and pearls. Shrouds, winding sheets and palls of Russian make are among the world's best examples of artistic needlework.

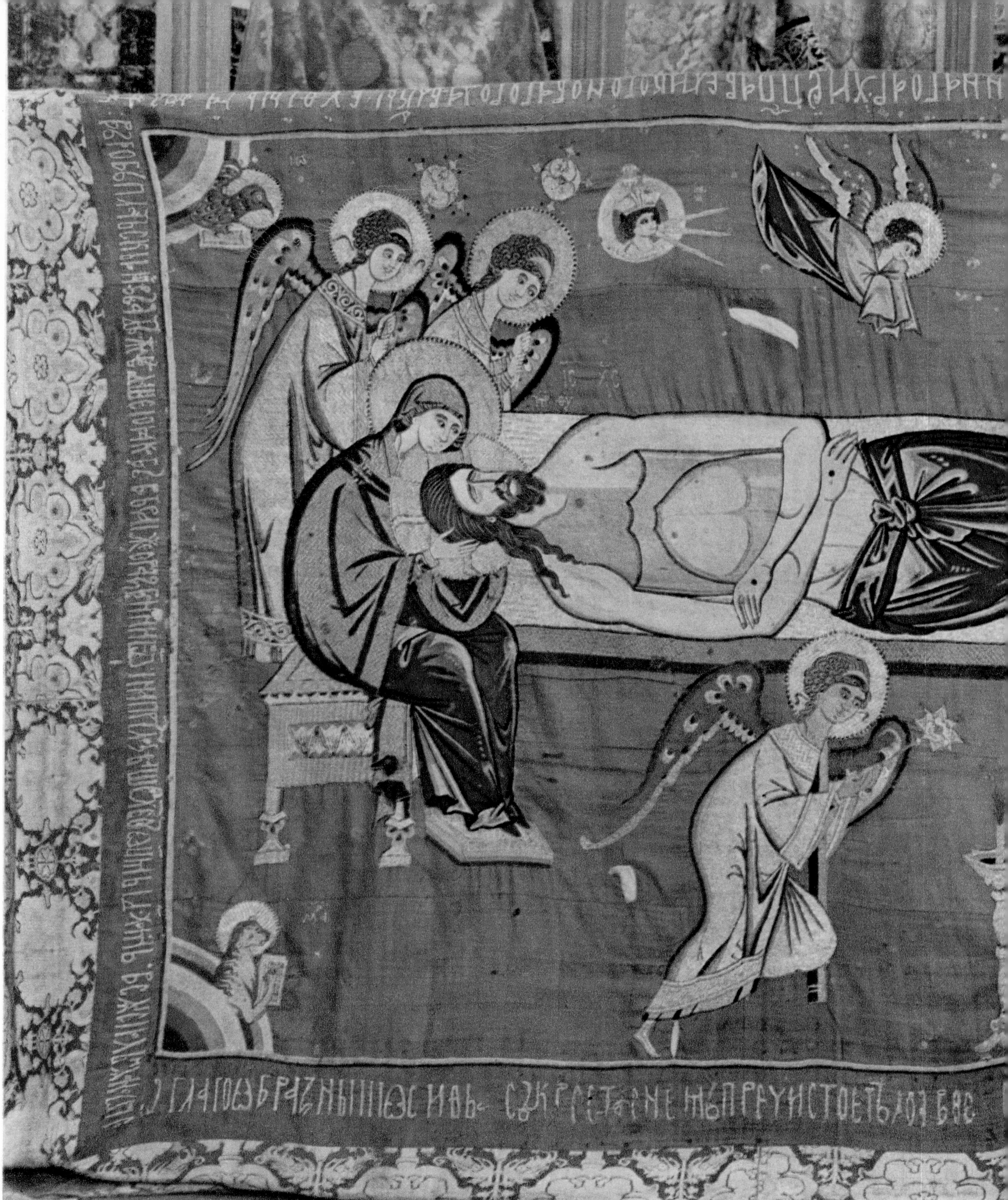

V. ANCIENT FABRICS AND COSTUMES

85

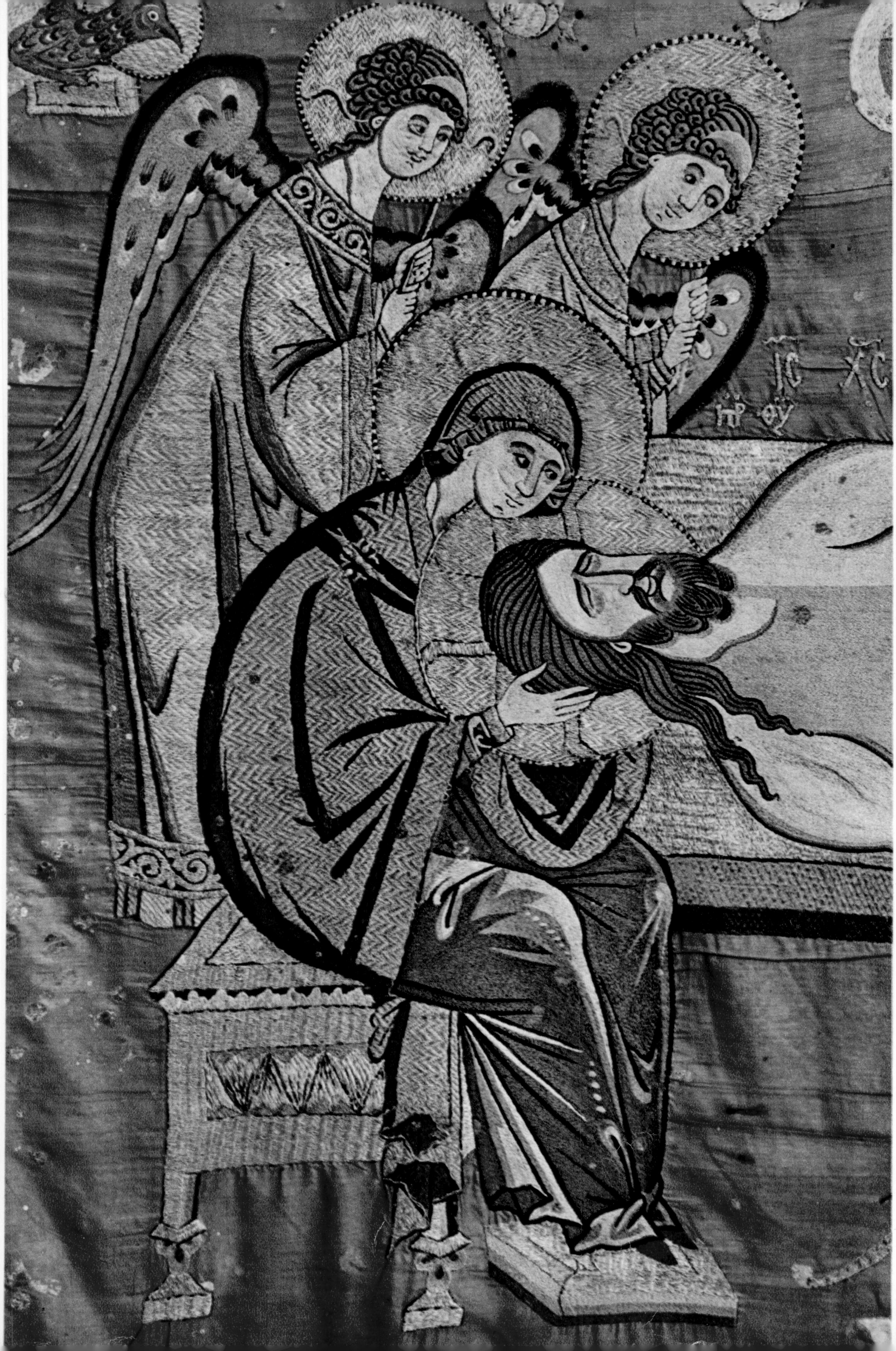
IC XC
MP ΘΥ

89

90

91

92

93

94

95

96

97

The custom of rulers exchanging valuable gifts at the conclusion of treaties of alliance or peace, or on completion of political negotiations, is a very ancient one. Russian ambassadorial or diplomatic etiquette regarded the offering of costly gifts as testimony of respect for the state concerned. On display at the Armoury are magnificent gifts from England, Poland, Denmark, Sweden, Holland, Austria and other countries. Each is a relic of the intricate diplomatic negotiations carried on in Moscow three or four centuries ago, while the collection as a whole is an impressive picture of the gradual extension of Russia's political and commercial ties and bears witness to her power and wealth.

The photographs show only a small part of the European silverware collected at the Armoury, including unique pieces made by 17th-century London craftsmen, superb Renaissance vessels from Hamburg and Nuremberg, sumptuous baroque objects made in Augsburg, and rare *objets d'art* from Paris. Even so, these pictures bring to life the pages of diplomatic history and illustrate the applied art of many countries.

VI. AMBASSADORIAL GIFTS

98

101

102

103

104

105

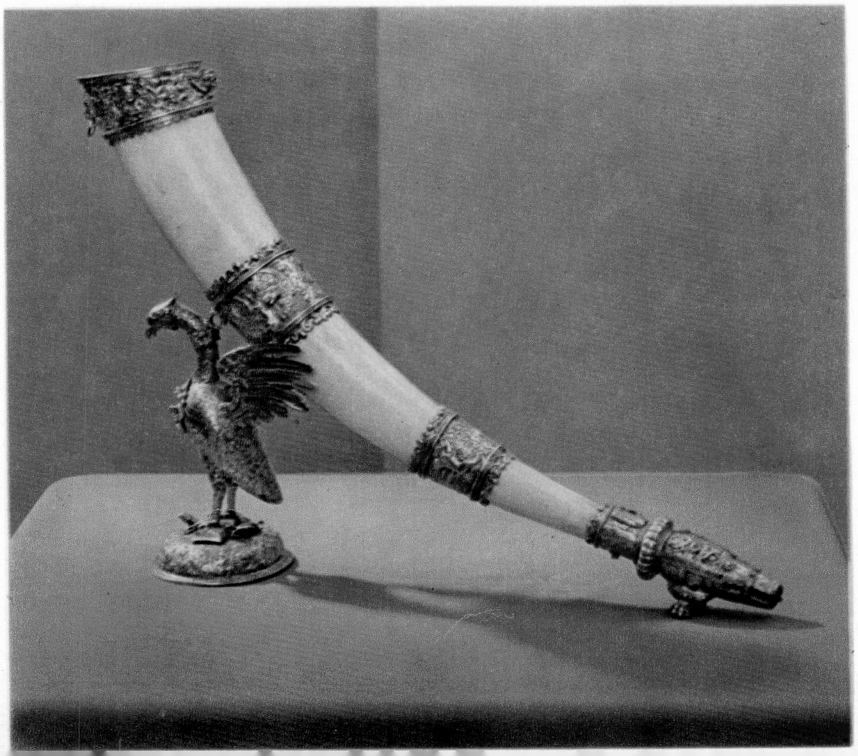

106

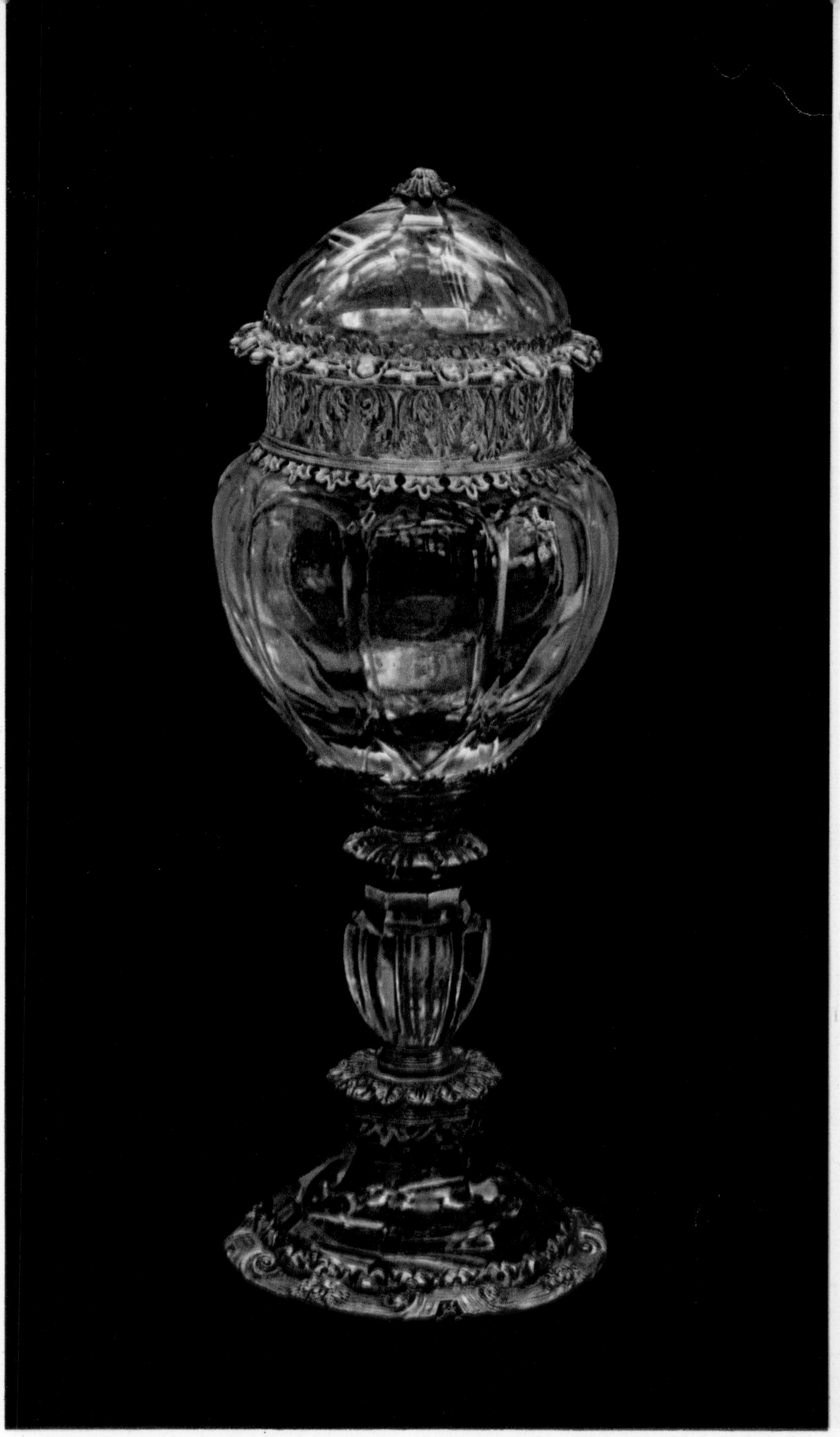

10

112

113

114

115

116

118

117

Notes on the Plates

120

1. The Armoury of the Moscow Kremlin.
2. View of the Kremlin across the Moskva River.
3. Openwork grille at the entrance to the exhibition halls on the ground floor.
4. Exhibition of Russian gold and silverware.
5. Lobby of the Armoury.
6. HELMET OF PRINCE YAROSLAV VSEVOLODOVICH. Hammered out of iron and ornamented with silver gilt repoussé work. Russian workmanship of the early 13th century. The museum's earliest piece of personal armour. Found in 1808 near the town of Yuriev-Polsky, on the bank of the Koloksha River, scene of the famous battle of Lipitsa, which was fought in 1216 by Konstantin and Georgy, the sons of Prince Vsevolod of Vladimir, for the grand-ducal title. Mstislav Udaloi was Konstantin's ally, and Yaroslav Vsevolodovich the ally of Georgy.
On the front plate of the helmet is an engraved niello inscription saying that its owner was Yaroslav Vsevolodovich. It is 20 cm. in diameter.
7—8. BYZANTINE 13th-CENTURY HELMET. Hammered out of iron in the form of a tall cone-shaped hat with broad, almost horizontal brim. Its surface is covered with a fine filigree grass ornament in silver and gold. The traditional holy images of Christ, the Virgin Mary, St John the Baptist, and the Archangels Michael and Gabriel are inlaid in gold along the broad crown of the helmet. These are followed by the figures of three prelates and two six-winged seraphim. Greek inscriptions to each figure are also done in fine gold and silver wire.
The helmet may have been acquired by the Treasury on the occasion of the arrival in Rus of the Greek Princess Sophia Paleologus, the wife of Ivan III.
The helmet is 30 cm. high, 22 cm. in diameter, and weighs 2.25 kg.
9—10. SPEARHEAD of the Tver Prince Boris Alexandrovich, and the detail of its sleeve socket. Made in Russia in the early 15th century. Forged Damascene steel; the sleeve is overlaid with silver leaf, with eight engraved scenes from the hunt and everyday life, and the following inscription: "The Spear of the Grand Prince Boris Alexandrovich." He ruled Tver from 1425 to 1461. The spear is listed in the main inventory of the royal armoury compiled in 1687; it may have been deposited in 1485 after the capture of Tver. The overall length of the spearhead is 46 cm.
11—12. DAMASCENED STEEL BUCKLER. Made in Iran in the 16th century. Belonged to F. I. Mstislavsky, a voivoda under Ivan the Terrible. Made of a piece of crucible steel of beautiful "water". Its surface is chased with a vortex of 42 strips of which each alternate one is polished and filled with gold. The only example of this kind of filling of Damascened steel with precious metal.
The encrusted patterns and the motifs of the foliation are highly varied: they include battle and hunting scenes, figures of men and animals in characteristic postures, ferocious lions, leopards and tigers, fleet-footed gazelles, mountain goats and stags. All are expressive and remarkably true to life. The label bears the inscription: "Made by Mūmin Mohammed — zerneshān (i.e. goldsmith)." The shield is 50.8 cm. in diameter and weighs 2.2 kg.
13. MANCHURIAN 17th-CENTURY STEEL HELMET. Ornamented in gold with inset coral, and gold-filled incised characters. A gift to Tsar Mikhail Fyodorovich Romanov from "the Tungus land", presented on October 28, 1638 by "laba" Irdenei-Dainmen Gerlandzu. The gilt openwork hemisphere at the top is terminated by a gilt chiselled tube for the plume. Weight: 1.2 kg.
14. HELMET AND VAMBRACES OF PRINCE F. I. MSTISLAVSKY, who is mentioned in historical records from 1571 to 1600. Sixteenth-century Iranian make. Damascened steel adorned with gold plates set with gems and turquoise; part of the boyar's parade armour worn by him on all his campaigns. Deposited at the royal treasury in 1622 upon the death of Prince Mstislavsky. Height of the helmet: 12 cm.; diameter: 21.4 cm.
15. GROUP OF RUSSIAN WARRIORS IN 16th-CENTURY ARMOUR. In the centre is Tsar Boris Godunov's "baidana", a coat of ring-mail. The warriors are armed with spears, maces and clubs, as well as swords and sabres, and wear helmets topped with long spikes dating from the 14th—16th centuries.
16. DETAIL OF TSAR BORIS GODUNOV'S COAT OF MAIL. Made of large flat rings engraved with the words: "God Is With Us; None Against Us." At the royal treasury since 1589. Weight: 6 kg.
17—18. MAIL-AND-PLATE COAT OF TSAR MIKHAIL FYODOROVICH made in 1620 by Konon Mikhailov of the Armoury.
The flaps and plates are covered with a fine gold tracery. The breast of the coat consists of five vertical rows of narrow overlapping plates and the back of seven rows. The coat is fastened at the side with silver clasps. Weight: 12 kg.
19—20. PLATE ARMOUR MADE IN 1663 BY NIKITA DAVYDOV OF THE ARMOURY. Consists of riveted steel plates. The chevron grooves on the plates are alternately gilt and silver. A double-headed eagle encircled by a laurel wreath is represented in the central breastplate. The gilt perimeter of the central plate is deeply incised. The plates are edged with silver fringes. The design and decoration suggest that the armour was made for ceremonial purposes.
Weight: 11.6 kg.
21. 17th-CENTURY "ALAM" (GUNNER'S BREASTPLATE) AND CANNON-BALLS. The breastplate was worn by gunners to distinguish them from common soldiers and *streltsy*. It was laced to their clothes by means of leather thongs. In the 17th century gunners were a privileged section of the Russian forces. Judging by the calibre, cannon fired whole shot weighing from one pound (400 grams) to 10 lb. and over. The cannon-balls were cast in earthen moulds consisting of two halves, or mould boxes.
22—23. HELMET OF TSAR MIKHAIL FYODOROVICH. Damascened steel, chiselled in polished facets and inlaid with gold ornament. The nosepiece bears a fine multicoloured enamel set with diamonds, rubies and emeralds. Made in 1621 by Nikita Davydov of the Armoury. Weight: 1.6 kg.
24. SABRE OF TSAR MIKHAIL FYODOROVICH, made in 1618 by Ilya Prosvit of the Armoury. Forged from Oriental steel with a texture of wavy lines, the blade is decorated with carving and inlay. Above the ornament on either side is an inscription in gold giving the name of the owner, the maker and the date it was made. The scabbard is covered with green velvet and overlaid with pierced silver gilt.
The sabre is 107 cm. long; weight without the scabbard: 1.48 kg.
25. SABRES OF THE HEROES of the Russian people's war of liberation from foreign intervention in 1612.
The sabre of Prince Dmitry Pozharsky is forged from Persian steel; a band running near the hilt bears the following inscription in Arabic: "Sultan Ali . . . The Work of Nuri, the Son of Ariser." The scabbard is covered with dark green leather and is mounted in silver gilt.
The sabre is 97 cm. long; weight without the scabbard: 960 grams.
The sabre of Kuzma Minin is forged from excellent Egyptian steel in an exceptionally simple design; it bears the following inscription: "The work of Master Ahmed of Cairo." The grip is of white bone,

the scabbard hangs from a simple red cord and is pasted over with black leather and decorated with iron figures. The sabre is 90 cm. long; weight without the scabbard: 860 grams.

26. SABRE MADE BY THE RUSSIAN CRAFTSMAN IVAN BUSHUYEV (Zlatoust Arms Factory, 1829), to mark the capture of the fortress of Varna from the Turks. The blade is gilt, burnished and ornamented with scenes of military operations at the siege of the fortress. On the blade is the inscription: "Varna, September 29, 1828."

The hilt is of ivory and the gilt guard is cast in the form of a Victory carrying a palm branch. Length of the sabre is 10.5 cm.; weight without the scabbard: 950 grams.

27–28. HARQUEBUS OF TSAR ALEKSEI MIKHAILOVICH made in 1654 by Grigory Vyatkin of the Armoury, according to the inscription on the barrel. It was used for hunting big game like the elk, wild boar and bear. The trigger is filed in the shape of a monster's head, and a hunting scene is cut on the plate of the gunlock.

The calibre of its rifled barrel is 18 mm.; total weight: 20 kg.; overall length: 1.51 m.

29. BUTT OF RUSSIAN 17th-CENTURY HARQUEBUS. The work of Martyn Chernorutsky of the Armoury.

The buttstocks and tipstocks of harquebuses were usually made of apple wood and ornamented with plates or inlays of coloured wood, ivory or mother-of-pearl engraved with animals, people, horsemen, birds and various vignettes. They were sometimes covered with lacquer or black paint. Length: 33 cm.; width: 10 cm.

30. PART OF THE ARMS EXHIBITION. A notable feature is the abundance of jewelled weapons.

In the centre is the *saadak* of Tsar Mikhail Fyodorovich's "great regalia" consisting of a bow case and quiver; above it is his plate armour made in 1616 by Konovalov; beyond them are some hunting harquebuses made by 17th-century Russian craftsmen of the Armoury, most of them with rifled barrels. Below are a number of Oriental daggers dating from the 17th and 18th centuries.

31. ORIENTAL 17th-CENTURY DAGGERS, with Damascened blades, hilts and scabbards overlaid with gold leaf and set with rubies, emeralds and diamonds. Apart from their purely historical value they are very costly, some priced at tens of thousands of gold rubles. Length of the blades is from 20 to 30 cm.

32. SAADAK (BOW CASE AND QUIVER) OF TSAR MIKHAIL FYODOROVICH'S "GREAT REGALIA". Made in 1628 by craftsmen of the Armoury. Ornamented with gold openwork and multicoloured enamel, and diamonds, rubies and emeralds. Special interest attaches to the heraldic figures of the eagle, lion, griffin, unicorn, etc. All are covered with a transparent coloured enamel. At royal processions, noblemen walked in front of the tsar carrying the *saadak*, together with other articles of the "great regalia" — the crown, sceptre and mound. Length of the bow is 72.8 cm.: width 28.5 cm.

33–34. THE CAP OF MONOMAKH, the earliest royal crown. Made of eight triangular golden plates on which is soldered a spiralling lace pattern of hair-fine gold wire. Six-petalled lotuses are picked out in filigree on four of the plates.

The origin of the Cap of Monomakh is obscure, although Russian and foreign scholars have made studies of it. It is now accepted that it was made by an Oriental craftsman in the late 13th or early 14th centuries. The appearance of the crown in Russia is connected with the legend which arose in the 15th century, in the reign of Ivan III, that the Byzantine Emperor Constantine IX, called Monomachus, sent regalia to his grandson, the Kiev Prince Vladimir Monomakh. In 1498, the Cap of Monomakh was first used in the coronation of Dmitry Ivanovich, a grandson of Ivan III. The last tsar to be crowned with it, in 1682, was Ivan Alekseyevich V, a brother of Peter the Great.

The summit of the cap with semi-precious stones and the cross, the gems on the faces, and the fur edging are of later origin; at any rate, the Cap already had its present form by the 17th century. It weighs 698 grams, and with the cross is 184 mm. high.

35. KAZAN CAP made in Moscow in the mid-16th century. First recorded in the treasury of Ivan the Terrible. The crown is covered with a fine grass pattern done on a niello background; it is ringed with three rows of "merlons" of varying size and shape in the form of flowers and ogee arches in a pierced foliation. The ornamentation, the luxuriant tracery on a niello background, and the choice of stones — turquoise and almandine — were typical of Oriental art, while the "merlons" in the form of arches and flowers were a popular motif of ancient Russian art.

It has been suggested that the Kazan Cap was made by order of Ivan the Terrible to mark the capture of Kazan in 1553. It is represented on G. Ugrimov's canvas, *Ivan the Terrible's Entry into Kazan*, which is at the State Russian Museum, and also on a Russian tapestry of similar name, on display at the Armoury. Height: 26.5 cm.; diameter: 21.5 cm.; weight; 1 kg. 963 grams.

36–37. IVORY THRONE OF TSAR IVAN THE TERRIBLE, an example of 16th-century Western art. It is a wooden chair with arms and back. The body is covered with ivory plates with carvings from history, mythology, heraldry and everyday life. When the throne was restored in the 17th century some spoiled plates were replaced; in 1856, a gilt eagle was attached to the back. It was used for coronations until the late 19th century, and is well known from M. Antokolsky's sculpture, *Ivan the Terrible*, on show at the State Tretyakov Gallery. Height: 1.37 m.; width: 61 cm.

38–39. THRONE OF TSAR BORIS GODUNOV, of late 16th-century Iranian make. The wooden body is overlaid with gold leaf stamped with a grass pattern *(basma)* and set with a great number of semi-precious stones, among which a delicate blue turquoise, the favourite stone of the East, predominates. Beneath the 18th-century upholstery is the original one of Iranian velvet dating back to the 16th century. In shape and ornament this is a typical example of 16th-century Iranian art. From 17th-century documents we learn that in 1604 it was brought by the Iranian Ambassador, Lachin-Beg, as a gift to Tsar Boris Godunov from Shah Abbas I. Height: 89 cm.; width: 61 cm.

40–41. "DIAMOND" THRONE OF TSAR ALEKSEI MIKHAILOVICH, made in Iran in the second half of the 17th century. The richest and most beautiful of all the thrones extant. It is skilfully adorned in several techniques (chasing, enamelling, polychrome painting, embroidery, pierced work) with the use of a variety of materials (silver, gold and fabrics).

The front is covered with enchased figures of elephants in a pierced foliation, and the sides with pierced tracery and magnificent coloured miniatures from everyday life.

The throne is dazzling because of the great many gems; among them are more than 800 diamonds from which it derives its name. It was made by special order and presented to Tsar Aleksei Mikhailovich by the company of Armenian traders in Iran. Height: 1 m. 53 cm.; width: 65 cm.

42. DIAMOND CROWN OF PETER THE GREAT, made in Moscow in 1682–89. The sparkling surface of the crown is an intricate pattern of flowers, double-headed eagles and crowns set in 800 large and small diamonds of superb cut. Here the diamond-

setter's skill takes pride of place. Height (with a cross): 29 cm.; diameter: 20 cm.; weight: 1 kg. 419.5 grams.

43. MOUND OF TSAR ALEKSEI MIKHAILOVICH ROMANOV. A big spherical orb surmounted by a Greek cross. Made in Constantinople in 1662 by Ivan Yuryev and brought to Moscow that same year. Its golden surface is adorned with a pattern of diamond, ruby and emerald flowers and fruits. The gems are set in low golden castings, with the space in between filled with a transparent emerald-green enamel. Like much that was made in 17th-century Constantinople, the mound reveals distinct features of Turkish art.

Height: 29 cm.; weight: 1.570 kg.

44. BEATEN SILVER CHALICE, a treasure of 12th-century Russian art. Made by craftsmen of Vladimir-Suzdal Rus, and presented by Prince Yuri Dolgoruky, the founder of Moscow, to the Cathedral of the Transfiguration in the town of Pereyaslavl-Zalessky.

Its design is simple and refined. The smooth surface is decorated with the images of saints and an inscription along the rim in a highly elegant style which is also characteristic of other Russian *objets d'art* of the period.

Height: 26 cm.; diameter of the cup: 19.5 cm.

45. GRAND-DUCAL COLLAR, worn over rich robes. Found in 1822 among the objects of the so-called "Ryazan treasure-trove" near the village of Staraya Ryazan.

Made by Kiev craftsmen in the 12th or 13th centuries, this chain is an excellent example of the finest two-tier filigree and cloisonné, at their peak in Ancient Rus in the pre-Mongolian period.

The diameter of the medallions ranges from 74 cm. to 80 cm.

46. PANAGIA, a medallion worn by ecclesiastics of the highest rank. A cameo with an image of the Crucifixion carved on two layers of onyx; the work of 12th-century Byzantine craftsmen. In the 16th century it was mounted by Moscow jewellers in a magnificent gold setting of jewels, pearls, and the finest filigree with fillets of coloured enamel. In 1589, this Panagia was conferred by Tsar Fyodor Ivanovich upon the first Patriarch of Rus, Iov, on the day of his consecration.

The cameo is 6.8 cm. by 6 cm.; the panagia, 15.8 cm. by 8.8 cm.

47–48. GOSPEL COVER (1499). In the 15th century, Moscow silversmiths were especially proficient in the ancient art of filigree. An excellent example of their work is this silver cover for a manuscript Gospel.

The filigree design, delicate and free, is executed in virtuoso style and covers the surface with a luxuriant network of lace. The main pattern is made of a smooth flattened wire, and the shoots and scrolls of a hairlike double-spun thread.

Linked by the filigree work are five cast and chased images in frames; against a green enamelled background are the Crucifixion (centre) and the four Evangelists (in the corners).

Size: 33 cm. by 22 cm.

49. CHASED SILVER CENSER (15th century) repeating an ancient Russian architectural type: a single-cupola temple in the form of a cube with two rows of corbelled *kokoshniki* arches on the walls. This censer is very similar in design to the Cathedral of the Annunciation in the Moscow Kremlin. Height: 28 cm.; diameter: 12.3 cm.; weight: 1 kg. 11 grams.

50. GOLD GOSPEL COVER (1571) set with large gems, mainly sapphires, and adorned with a filigree ornament filled in with pastel enamels: white, green and blue of many shades. The "zern", tiny drops of gold and miniature bunches of grapes sprinkled over the decorated surface, add greatly to its richness. The Gospel is one of the finest monuments of 16th-century decorative art, and is unsurpassed in the richness, beauty and harmony of its enamels. Size: 27 cm. by 43 cm.

51. GREAT SILVER DIPPER made in 1535 by craftsmen of the Moscow Kremlin. It was owned by Prince I. I. Kubensky, and is an excellent example of silversmith's work of the first half of the 16th century. The bottom is in the form of shallow fluting converging at the centre. On the handle is a cast pierced ornament: an animal fighting a winged serpent in the midst of grass.

The dipper is very simple in design; its ornament and shape, characteristic of the period, create an impression of repose.

Length with spout: 41.7 cm.

At feasts, mead, a popular drink, was offered in dippers, a national form of vessel in ancient Rus.

52. HEAVY ORNAMENTAL DIPPER made in 1618 from a piece of gold, richly adorned with pearls, gems and niello, by craftsmen of the Gold Hall of the Moscow Kremlin. It was presented to Tsar Mikhail Romanov by his mother, Marfa Ivanovna.

Weight: 1.2515 kg.

53. BRATINA, a silver gilt goblet dating from the first half of the 17th century, skilfully chased with a freely weaving foliation on a stippled surface.

It was given to the inventor Mikhail Danilov, for "services to the tsar".

The *bratina* is a goblet for drinking mead, beer or kvass. At feasts a big *bratina* was used as a loving cup. Passed round from guest to guest it was a symbol uniting them into a single family and making them friends and brothers. Hence the name of *bratina*, which stems from the root "*brat*", brother. Diameter: 13.3 cm.; weight: 628.9 grams.

54. SOLID GOLD CHALICE (1664) covered with coloured enamel and jewels. It was made by Kremlin craftsmen by order of the wife of boyar Morozov, Anna Ilyinichna, and was her donation to the Chudov Monastery of the Kremlin.

Excellent workmanship, elegant ornamentation and the harmony of bright multicoloured enamels with emeralds, rubies, sapphires and diamonds make the chalice an outstanding example of 17th-century art. Height: 28 cm.; diameter of the chalice: 18.5 cm.; weight: 2.3145 kg.

55. GOLD CUP, with spoon-like fluting, adorned with multicoloured enamel and gems. In 1694, it was given by Peter the Great to his son Prince Aleksei. Diameter: 15.4 cm.; weight: 426.5 grams.

56. GOLD CASING OF THE ICON "COMPASSION", dating from the first third of the 17th century. Framed in a foliated enamel decoration and gems, the icon is set in a chased silver triptych which belonged to Ivan Gryazev, State Secretary of the Diplomatic Office. The painting's harmony with the multicoloured enamels set off by the thick foliage raised in relief, the soft glow of silver, gold, pearls and gems, is a fascinating sight. The long pearl pendants descending from the halo recall the ancient head-dress of princesses and royal brides.

57. USOLYE ENAMELS made in Solvychegodsk in the second half of the 17th century. A characteristic feature of Usolye enamels is the peculiar arrangement of colours — blue, green and light yellow — on a snow-white background, and the use of hatching, which looks very much like etching, to convey the impression of shade. The motifs of the ornaments are varied: bright tulips on long stalks with leaves, sunflowers, mayweed, poppies, scenes from Russian folk tales, and allegorical and biblical subjects.

58. GOSPEL COVER ADORNED WITH USOLYE ENAMEL. Usolye craftsmen were masters of the art of filigree, which they

used to secure enamel plaques to surfaces. They also used it as a characteristic framework for various ornamental motifs. Height: 47 cm.; width: 29 cm.; weight: 9 kg. 855 grams.

59. MANUSCRIPT GOSPEL of 1678, illuminated with 1,200 miniatures in colour, a great number of vignettes, headpieces, tailpieces and ornamental capital letters. According to the chronicle, seven artists of the Armoury, Fyodor Zubov, Ivan Maksimov, Sergei Vasilyev, Pavel Nikitin, Fyodor Yuryev, Makar Potapov and Maksim Ivanov, worked "eight months day and night" to illuminate the Gospel. They treated the religious subjects in a lively style with scenes from everyday life and fairy-tale episodes. Height: 97.5 cm.; width: 34.5 cm.; weight: 19 kg. 700 grams.

60–61. GOLDEN COVER FOR MANUSCRIPT GOSPEL of 1678 done by a group of Russian and foreign artists of the Gold Hall of the Moscow Kremlin, including Mikhail Vasilyev, Dmitry Terentiev and the enameller Yuri Frobos.

Here the work of the goldsmith is in perfect harmony with that of the enameller, who has covered the images done in high relief with a bright polychrome enamel. The glitter of gold goes exceedingly well with the transparent and opaque enamels, which vie with the sparkle of the many emeralds, sapphires and rubies.

62. GREAT SILVER GILT CHALICE made in 1685 in the town of Nizhny Novgorod (now Gorky).

The bowl is overlaid with a pierced pattern of fantastic flowers, heightened by cast figures of cherubim, symbols of angels and allegories of the four elements: earth, water, air and fire.

The embossed ornament is rich and massive and recalls carving in wood.

63. SILVER BOWL WITH LID AND TUMBLER made in 1685 for the Princess Sofia Alekseyevna by craftsmen of the Silver Hall of the Moscow Kremlin, Mikhail Mikhailov and Andrei Pavlov. It was apparently used for fruit drinks, fresh berries and jams.

The massive silver tumbler, like the bowl, is adorned with incised gilt ornament of grass and flowers freely arranged against a dark unbroken network of fine niello tracery and flowers. Height: 13.2 cm.; weight: 348.7 grams.

64. SILVER PLATE WITH NIELLO WORK made in Moscow in the second half of the 17th century. It belonged to the nobleman Bogdan Khitrovo, who was in charge of the Armoury and the Gold and Silver Halls of the Moscow Kremlin. The rim resembles petals, alternately gilt and nielloed, with an ornament of flowers and foliage. In the centre are Khitrovo's arms: a hand holding a sword crossed by two sabres. Width: 28.6 cm.; weight: 586.1 grams.

65. DIPPER of 1755 made of silver gilt in the form of a boat with a flat bottom. In place of the handle and the lip are carved and cast silver figures of eagles with crowns. On the bottom is a disc bearing an embossed image of a double-headed eagle. Along the outer rim are four embossed rococo cartouches with the following inscription: "This dipper . . . is awarded to the Collegiate Assessor Kozma Matveyev for his zeal in augmenting the revenue of the Crown, and his conscientiousness." In the 18th century, such dippers were awarded for "loyal service" to rent collectors as well as to Cossack chieftains. Height: 22.5 cm.; length: 46 cm.; width: 20.5 cm.; weight: 2 kg. 700 grams.

66. GOLD REVOLVING CLOCK WITH SPRAY OF LILIES. The white enamelled face of the clock in the form of a circlet around the vase rotates, while the diamond arrow-head is static. The egg-shaped body is covered with a transparent yellow enamel, the elegant lilies are of onyx, their petals of brilliants, and the stamens and stems of coloured gold. The clock was made in 1899 by the Russian craftsman M. Perkhin, who worked for the firm of Fabergé in Petersburg. Height: 26.5 cm.; length: 9.7 cm.; width: 6.3 cm.

67. FLAT OVAL GILT SNUFF-BOX. On its lid, covered with a transparent red enamel, is a half-length portrait of Peter the Great done by Andrei Ovsov, one of the first Russian miniaturists to work in enamels. He was a pastmaster of enamelling and made a series of miniatures of Peter the Great, which were presented to members of his retinue. Ovsov's miniatures are distinguished for singular purity and lustre of colour and lucidity of design. Height: 2.3 cm.; length: 9.2 cm.; width: 5.3 cm.

68. GOLD CLOCKWORK MODEL OF SIBERIAN TRAIN WITH PLATINUM ENGINE. On the carriages are inscriptions visible through a magnifying glass, reading: "Trans-Siberian Line", "Ladies", "Smoking Car", "Chapel", etc. The windows are of crystal and the engine has a ruby lantern. In the engine is a starting switch. It packs away in a silver egg on an onyx stand. On the egg is engraved a map of the Siberian Railway with the inscription "The Great Siberian Railway in 1900". Made in 1900 in Petersburg by M. Perkhin and his apprentice Y. Nikolai. The dimensions of the egg: 27.2 cm. × 12.8 cm.; the dimensions of the train: 39.8 cm. × 1.4 cm.; weight: 2 kg. 99.7 grams.

69. MODEL OF THE FIRST-CLASS CRUISER "PAMYAT AZOVA" OF THE BALTIC FLEET. A replica of the ship in gold and platinum on an aquamarine base resembling the sea. Encased in an egg of bloodstone. The surface of the egg is adorned with an appliqué gold ornament in rococo style raised upon the dark-green background. The dimensions of the egg: 9.3 cm. × 7.6 cm.; the dimensions of the cruiser: 4.9 cm. × 7.8 cm. × 4.8 cm.; weight: 466.4 grams.

Made by M. Perkhin and Y. Nikolai in 1891.

70. SADDLES OF RUSSIAN 16th-CENTURY MAKE. The saddle from the time of Ivan the Terrible (in the foreground) is covered with embroidered cherry-coloured velvet and jewelled gold plates. Boris Godunov's saddle (in the background) dating from 1600, has a silver lining with a hairline engraving of flowers and birds, and embossed lions' heads on the saddle-bow. The decoration underlines the beauty of its form. The metal cover was made in Lübeck and later embossed and engraved by Russian craftsmen.

71. SADDLE OF TSAR MIKHAIL FYODOROVICH, made by the Moscow craftsman Ivan Popov "with comrades". Covered with beaten gold and adorned with polychrome enamels whose bright hues harmonise with the glitter of the many gems, among them diamonds, sapphires and emeralds. The massive proportions of the saddle are enhanced by the intricate ornamentation. The seat and skirts are covered with velvet, the most costly fabric at the time. The saddle took almost two years to make: 1637 and 1638.

72. SADDLE OF RUSSIAN WORKMANSHIP OF THE SECOND HALF OF THE 17th CENTURY. The goldwork is adorned with a dazzling green enamel covered with a pattern of grape-vines, and set off with large sapphires, emeralds and diamonds, in a highly pleasing colour scheme. The seat is embroidered with flowers in pearls and emeralds. The costly decoration is reminiscent of Oriental saddles but in shape it is a Russian "archak". The typically Russian rounded scallops and the pearl trimming of the seat are indications that the saddle was made in Moscow. It was apparently made for Tsar Fyodor's steed, for he was a great lover of ceremonial cavalcades.

73. "ARCHAK" (SADDLE) IN FILIGREE WORK, made in 1682 by Luka Mymrin, Stepan Fedotov and Larion Afanasyev of Moscow. A filigree foliation of leaves, flowers and grasses enamelled in blue, light green, and white, with almost the appearance of coloured lace.

74. DECORATIVE HARNESS made in China in the second half of the 17th century. The saddles are adorned with coloured mother-of-pearl, carved gilt bronze and sky-blue enamel. The cloths are made of satin and velvet, embroidered in gold and coloured silks. The clouds and dragons are represented with great skill. These objects were brought from China in 1678 by Ambassador Nikolai Spafari, who travelled to China for trade.

75. DECORATIVE HARNESS made by Polish and German craftsmen of the 16th and 17th centuries. The saddle in the centre, by Andreas Mackensen, has a very high pommel and cantle, and is intended for a heavily armed rider. It is covered with velvet and adorned with handsome raised embroidery. Large tulips with leaves in spun silver (metal thread spun with silk) look like live flowers. Polish saddles (on the left) have pieces of engraved silverwork on them. They were presented by King Sigismund III of Poland to Tsar Boris Godunov in 1600. Saddles of this type, known as "hussar", have been preserved only at the Armoury.

76. COACH HALL with a reconstruction of an 18th-century royal cavalcade. In the 18th and 19th centuries, from six to eight richly caparisoned horses drew each vehicle, with dozens of gilded carriages following the royal coach.

77–79. ENGLISH COACH OF THE LATE 16th CENTURY, the museum's oldest equipage. It has blinds instead of glass panes, and lacks both springs and turn-table. The body is suspended on straps. The armchairs inside are upholstered in Iranian velvet, and the sides in Italian velvet. The coach is made entirely of oak, and is adorned with sculptured carvings and paintings. On the front is a scene of a battle between Christians and Moslems on the outskirts of a town in the centre of which rises a tower. To the right is the Moslem army led by a turbaned horseman in a caftan of gold fabric. To the left is the Christian army. At its head is a horseman in the act of spearing the enemy's horse. The horseman and the other knights are clad in heavy coats of mail.

On the sides are scenes in bold relief carving of bear, wild boar and tiger hunting, apparently in some tropical country. The carving on the coach is painted. On its boards are picturesque landscapes with parks and palaces.

The coach was presented by Queen Elizabeth I of England to Tsar Boris Godunov in 1603, and was remodelled for the reception of the Polish Embassy in 1678. In Russia this type of coach was called "kolymaga".

It is five metres long and over two metres wide.

80. CHILD'S COVERED SLEIGH. Made by Kremlin craftsmen. Belonged to Peter the Great when he was three years old. Upholstered in red leather embossed with golden flowers, it has an improved turn-table.

The memoirs of contemporaries say that ponies were used to pull the sleigh. Peter was accompanied by four dwarfs, the smallest of them riding behind on a tiny pony.

Length: about 1.5 m.; height: about 1 m.; width: 65 cm.

81. TRAVELLING SLEIGH MADE IN PETERSBURG IN 1742. The body has four doors and 10 windows. Inside are a table and benches covered with green cloth. The outside is gilt, coloured and carved.

In this sleigh the Empress Yelizaveta made the three-day journey from Petersburg for her coronation in Moscow. It was pulled by 23 horses: one pair and seven troikas.

Length: 6 m.; height: 2 m.; width: 2 m.

82. COACH MADE BY BOURNIHALL OF PARIS (1757). A present from the Hetman of the Ukraine, K. G. Razumovsky, to Empress Yelizaveta. Adorned with a magnificent rococo carving in wood, the scrolls resembling the foam and spray of the sea. The painting is by François Boucher. The coach has not been restored and remains in its original state.

Length: 9 m.; height: 3 m.; width: 2.5 m.

83–84. SUMMER COACH OF CATHERINE II (THE GREAT). A gondola-type two-seater with roof and folding cover. Made in 1779 by English craftsmen. It is remarkable for its carving in wood: the body is adorned with wreaths of flowers, foliage and banners. The box is supported by eagles with extended wings. On the back are figures of horsemen spearing dragons. Under a great carved shell is the figure of Poseidon holding an oar. A gilt laurel branch trims the roof of the gondola; it is carved of maple wood but creates the impression of a metal casting. On the body against a gilt background are paintings in the style of the Boucher school. Some of the compositions are by Russian artists. Length: 4.5 m.; height: 2.5 m.; width: about 2 m.

85. VESTMENT OF METROPOLITAN PYOTR made in 1322 of light-blue Byzantine satin interwoven with golden stripes and encircled crosses. The combination of blue and gold lends the fabric a dignified beauty.

Fabrics adorned with crosses were used mainly for the vestments of the highest order of clergy. On icons, frescoes and palls the saints and patriarchs are depicted in vestments made of such fabrics. Metropolitan Pyotr is shown wearing his vestment on an icon by Dionisy, the well-known Russian 15th-century artist, in the Cathedral of the Assumption in the Moscow Kremlin, and also on the pall of 1519 made by order of the Moscow Grand Prince Vasily III (now at the Armoury).

The vestment of 1322 is the oldest fabric in the Armoury.

86–87. THE "PUCHEZH WINDING SHEET" is the earliest example of Russian decorative needlework in the Armoury. It was made in 1441 by order of the Novgorod Archbishop Yevfimy, according to a silver thread text running along the border. It derives its name from the town of Puchezh, Ivanovo Region, where it was made. The embroidery is done on a light-crimson taffeta with multicoloured silks, and only the nimbuses and the attire of the angels are done in spun gold and silver. There is austerity in the simple composition and excellent taste in the selection of the silks which are harmonised into a remarkably soft but striking colour scheme.

Like 15th-century Russian painters, embroiderers favoured graceful elongated figures of elegant proportions, with softly rounded faces, frail hands and luxuriant hair falling to the shoulders in large curls. Ancient Russian embroiderers were justly called painters with the needle.

88. SLEEVE OF VESTMENT OF METROPOLITAN PYOTR (1322). An example of Russian 14th-century embroidery. Its design is severe and the material unpretentious. The main part consists of silver gilt plaques in the form of 'shrines' with embossed images of the saints. They are arranged in a row and alternate with plain narrow plaques of similar shape. All are threaded with small fresh-water pearls and heightened with small pearl crosses. The cuff is edged with a band of small round and square spangles in a pearl frame.

89–90. VESTMENT OF METROPOLITAN DIONISY made in 1583 of a rare 16th-century Oriental satin by order of Ivan the Terrible in memory of his murdered son, Prince Ivan.

The collar, sleeves and borders of the vestment are excellent examples of Russian embroidery of the late 16th century. The decoration is composed of rosettes, done in small fresh-water pearls, beautiful clusters of enamel, and large golden plaques in the form of 'shrines' made of gold with a fine niello tracery. The lettering on the borders makes a beautiful decorative pattern. It says: "By order of His Majesty the Tsar and Grand Prince Ivan Vasilyevich... this vestment has been made for the Metropolitan Dionisy at the Sacred Cathedral Church of the Most Holy Mother of God in Memory of his Son, the True Believer, Tsarevich and Grand Prince Ivan . . . The year of 7091, March, the 30th Day."

91. 17th-CENTURY SECULAR ROBES, full length, with wide sleeves, covering the human frame entirely. Those in the photograph are royal costumes. In the foreground is the state caftan of Peter the Great made of Italian gold brocade. According to the fashion of the time it is adorned with fine hand-made gold-and-silver lace.

92. MITRE OF THE FIRST HALF OF THE 17th CENTURY. On a background of light-blue velvet are gold plaques adorned with diamonds, rubies and emeralds, or with enamelled images of the saints. All are threaded with large and medium-sized pearls. Below, framed in enamelled pillars, are gold icons with enamelled images of Christ, the Virgin and St John the Baptist, arranged under arches in the customary style. On the rim of the mitre is a smooth gold plate with the following donative inscription executed in niello in intricate Slavonic letters: "In the year of 1634 by order of His Majesty and Grand Prince Mikhail Fyodorovich . . . this Hat has been made for the Cathedral Church in Rostov . . . in Memory of his Father . . . the Most Holy Patriarch Filaret Nikitich."

93. DETAIL OF VESTMENT OF PATRIARCH NIKON (1654). The vestment is made of Italian double-looped brocade, the most expensive fabric in the 17th century. Raised spun gold made the fabric very handsome and costly. The collar, sleeves, orphrey and borders are adorned with 16th-century Russian embroidery. The design is beautiful and the materials costly: large pearls, gems and gold plaques, superb niello miniatures with compositions of many figures and handsome clear-cut lettering.

Altogether the vestment is covered with almost 16 kg. of valuables. Its total weight is 24 kg.

The 1654 vestment gives a good idea of coronation caftans, none of which has come down to us.

94. 1742 CORONATION DRESS OF EMPRESS YELIZAVETA (daughter of Peter the Great). Farthingales came to Russia from France in the mid-18th century. Hoops were as wide as 1.5 metres, this style of dress being in the spirit of the fanciful rococo style which was then in fashion. Yelizaveta's state dress is representative of this. It is made of glazed silver brocade and adorned with gold lace. Displayed with the dress is a rare mantle of 18th-century crocheted silver lace.

95. DRESS OF THE FIRST QUARTER OF THE 18th CENTURY. This is the first ladies' dress in the European style after Peter's reforms. It is made of cherry-coloured silk and adorned with superb silver embroidery. In contrast to Russian dresses of the time, it is very low-necked; it consists of a bodice with short sleeves, a skirt and a train. Empress Catherine I wore it at her coronation in 1724, after which it was placed for safe-keeping at the Armoury.

96. GOLD SNUFF-BOX ornamented with transparent enamel, made in Paris in 1763 or 1764. Weight: 112.5 grams.

French mid-18th-century SPY-GLASS. Made of dark-green jasper, overlaid with a rococo gold pattern; the monograms are in brilliants and rubies. Length: 10.6 cm.; weight: 123.5 grams.

97. PETERSBURG TAPESTRY (1734). A type of decorative napless carpet done in the Gobelin technique. Made by hand from coloured drawings, often by well-known artists. In Russia, such tapestry was made from 1717 to 1859; its manufacture flourished in the second half of the 18th century when mainly Russian weavers were employed at the tapestry works. They produced hangings of excellent quality and fine artistic finish. Thousands of shades of wool and silk were used. Even very experienced weavers could not produce more than 1.5 metres a year. Dimensions: 2 m. 84 cm. × 2 m. 11 cm.

98. SILVER GILT STANDING CUP AND COVER made in 1612–13 by Robert Brook of London. Height: 89 cm.; weight: 6.469 kg.

The great bowl is embossed with a bold decoration in low relief in the middle of which are grotesque harpies.

99. SILVER GILT JUG made in England in 1604–05. Brought in 1620 for Tsar Mikhail Fyodorovich by the English Ambassador, John Merrick. The globular body is covered with a continuous embossed decoration. In two oval cartouches are sea monsters in waves. Height: 19 cm.; weight: 3 kg. 823.5 grams.

SILVER GILT CUP made in London in 1557–58. May have been brought for Tsar Ivan the Terrible by the merchant adventurer Anthony Jenkinson. This is the earliest piece of English workmanship at the Armoury. Height: 15 cm.; diameter 17 cm.; weight: 894.7 grams.

100. SILVER GILT HERALDIC PANTHER made in London in 1600–01. Weight: 29–34 kg.; height: 71 cm. A magnificent sculptured tankard of unique artistic value. The movable head is the lid. In the panther's forepaws is an ornately embossed shield. There is another similar sculptured panther at the Armoury; both were brought in 1629 together with a great quantity of other silverware by the English commercial agent Fabian Ulyanov.

101. SILVER GILT FLASK made in London in 1580–81. Brought to Moscow in 1604 by the English Ambassador, Sir Thomas Smith, as a present for Tsar Boris Godunov from King James I. This is a wine vessel of rare shape and ornamentation. There are only nine such vessels of English make known, six of them being at the Armoury. Height: 44 cm.; weight: 2 kg. 972.5 grams.

102. SILVER GILT SALT made in London in 1594–95. Its surface is covered with a continuous raised pattern in the midst of which are figures of Mars, Venus, Diana and Mercury in typical 16th-century attire, and also hunting scenes, masks, half-length figures, etc. Height: 41.5 cm.; weight: 1 kg. 327.5 grams.

103. SILVER GILT WINE JUG made in London in 1615–16, probably by Robert Brook. There are three other similar jugs at the Armoury. One of them was also made in 1615–16 and is exactly like the one in the photograph. The other two date from 1604–05. No other museum or private collection has such jugs. They are magnificent, massive and highly ornate in design, with cast fittings which were very rare in English silverwork. The jugs were brought to Moscow, together with the panthers, by the English commercial agent Fabian Ulyanov in 1629. Height: 62 cm.; weight: 8 kg. 343 grams.

104. SILVER GILT EAGLE made by the famous Nuremberg goldsmith Christopher Jamnitzer (1563–1618). Until 1628 it was in the treasury of King Christian IV of Denmark. After the Danish army's disasters in the Thirty Years War, it was pawned by the King with other silverware. In 1628, it was taken to Archangel, bartered for raw silk and brought to the Kremlin. The eagle is a large decorative wine vessel weighing almost 12 kg. Height: 51 cm.; wing span 89 cm.

105–106. IVORY DRINKING HORN. The setting consists of silver gilt rings and a chiselled cast figure of a bird to support the horn. An excellent piece of workmanship in the late Renaissance style by the outstanding German jeweller and silversmith Jacob Mores the Elder, who lived in Hamburg in the second half of the 16th century and the early 17th century. The Armoury has the world's largest collection of his works. Length: 62 cm.; weight: 1 kg. 881 grams.

107. CUP IN THE FORM OF A COCK. Late Gothic silver wine vessel made in Germany in the late 15th century. It belonged to the Grand Prince Ivan III of Moscow. The cock's head is movable. On its throat is a round green enamelled plate with the gilt inscription: "The Grand Prince Ivan Vasilyevich." Height: 32 cm.; weight: 1 kg. 569.7 grams.

108. ROCK-CRYSTAL CUP IN SILVER GILT SETTING. A remarkably harmonious Renaissance vessel, the only extant piece of work of the Nuremberg goldsmith Albrecht Jamnitzer. Made in 1550—55. This may be the magnificent cup of rock-crystal which was presented by Prince I. A. Khvorostinin to Dmitry the Usurper on May 16, 1606, the day of his marriage with Marina Mnishek. Height: 22 cm.; weight: 678 grams.

109. SILVER GILT SALVER made by Hans Braband of Nuremberg (1535—69). A very interesting piece of German silverwork of the mid-16th century. It entailed the use of repoussé, incising, carving, etc. The silversmith, skilled in each, made use of the wealth of patterns produced for silversmiths and jewellers by 16th-century German artists. Six discs in mother-of-pearl are set in the bottom. In the centre of each is a high stud adorned with varicoloured enamels and set with diamonds and rubies. Diameter: 46.2 cm.; weight: 4 kg. 147 grams.

110. CHINESE PORCELAIN CUP ON A CORAL STEM. The base is made of silver gilt by J. Bang, who worked in Nuremberg in the first third of the 17th century. It is in the form of a mountain crowded with cast figurines of a shepherd, horsemen, animals, etc. It was presented by King Christian IV of Denmark to Tsar Mikhail Fyodorovich in 1644. Height: 29 cm.; weight: 816.5 grams.

111. HERCULES SUPPORTING A CELESTIAL GLOBE, made in silver by Jacob Mores the Younger of Hamburg (1606—49), brought to Moscow on December 18, 1655, by the Swedish Ambassador Gustav Bjelke as a present from King Charles X to Tsar Aleksei Mikhailovich. The constellations and planets are engraved on both hemispheres. The ornate base is adorned with baroque scrollwork. There are three other rare silver globes at the Armoury dating from the 17th century. Height: 71 cm.; weight: 5 kg. 338.8 grams.

112—113. OVAL SILVER GILT SALVER, possibly the work of David Bessmann, a 17th-century craftsman of Augsburg. It was brought to Moscow for Tsar Aleksei Mikhailovich by the Polish Ambassador Kiprean in 1671. Its rim is covered with a large scrollwork decoration. In the centre is an embossed composition depicting Alexander the Great speaking to Diogenes in his tub. The Armoury has a large collection of 17th-century Augsburg salvers which were hung on the walls of the ancient Kremlin halls on state occasions and holidays. Length: 52.8 cm.; width: 44 cm.; weight: 1 kg. 193.5 grams.

114—115. SILVER GILT SALVER WITH SILVER GILT EWER. Interesting examples of French casting of the 17th century. They were made in 1649 by René Cousinet of Paris and brought to Moscow in 1664 by Charles Howard, Earl of Carlisle, the Ambassador of King Charles II of England, for Tsar Aleksei Mikhailovich. The salver and the ewer are a rarity, because in the late 17th and early 18th centuries a great quantity of French silverware was minted into money by order of King Louis XIV to replenish the royal treasury. Salver: 73.2 cm. in diameter; weight: 10 kg. 150 grams. Ewer: height: 45 cm.; weight: 4 kg. 408.2 grams.

116. SALVER AND EWER made in Augsburg in the second half of the 17th century. Brought to Moscow from Vienna in 1675 by the Austrian Emperor's ambassadors, Annibale Francesco di Bottoni and Johann Carl Terlinger. Made of round and oval polished panes of rock-crystal held in a silver gilt setting with enamel cabochons and clusters of gems: turquoise, amethyst, topaz and garnet. Salver: 64 cm. in diameter; weight: 4 kg. 40 grams. Ewer: height: 41.8 cm.; weight: 1 kg. 875.2 grams.

117—118. CRYSTAL WINE JAR made in the early 18th century by Frantz Gondelach, the famous Hessian glass-cutter. May have been ordered as a present for Peter the Great on his visit to Denmark in 1716. Height: 46 cm.

119. EAGLE MADE IN JAPAN in the 19th century. Its plumage consists of almost 2,000 ivory leaves of varying size and shape. Its wing-spread is 1.62 m. The base is the large stump of an old tree. On one of the tail feathers is the inscription: "Tokyo. Kanedo-Kanjiro."

A double-sided screen serves as a background for the eagle. In coloured silks on one side is a picture of rolling breakers and, on the other, hovering birds against a sunset.

The eagle and the screen were presented to the Russian Emperor in 1896. A similar eagle, also made in Japan, but sitting on the trunk of a tree, is in the New York Museum.

120. View of the exhibition halls on the first floor of the Museum.

List of Plates